Praise for *This Is Personal*

"Brennan and I go way back. Before I started ConvertKit, he and I would regularly host workshops that taught creators the business of selling online. He's been living and breathing this stuff for more than a decade, and *This Is Personal* lays out the perfect framework for meeting your ideal customers where they are today, and then using the magic of email automation to bring them to the point of being ready to buy from you. For anyone who's looking to sell more using email, this book is for you."

—Nathan Barry, Founder & CEO of ConvertKit

"I've been following Brennan for years; he's the master of email marketing and getting the very most out of your email list. This book is practical and instantly implementable. Brennan lays the foundation of doing email the right way while also giving advanced strategies to do more. I've already seen results since applying his strategies and I have so much more work to do. Thanks for creating such an incredible resource. No-brainer buy!"

—Cathryn Lavery, Founder of BestSelf

"I love how Brennan has created a framework that is both extremely modern but also evergreen for years to come. We've built our entire business on that framework, from the overall philosophy to the email templates to the personalization tools to his approach to automation, and I don't know of a more powerful way to tackle the opportunity that email marketing represents. Everyone who is trying to sell something online effectively needs to pick up this book and absorb everything it has to offer."

—Tiago Forte, author of *Building a Second Brain*

"Brennan has long been known by email marketers as THE authority on email personalization. His experience and success in the field have helped deliver results exceptional for creators like me. And now, with *The Is Personal*, he's delivered a comprehensive guide on how you can see these business-changing results, too. If email is part of your strategy (and it should be) this book should be required reading."

—Jay Clouse, Founder of Creator Science

"In his 1999 letter, Jeff Bezos wrote, 'We listen to customers, invent on their behalf, personalize the story for each of them, and earn their trust.'

I've been using email professionally since 2003 to build durable relationships with audiences, listening to them, then 'inventing' on their behalf. But while email has become a ubiquitous tool for creators, using email automation to create 'human level' personalization, as Brennan teaches, is not easy. Which is why 99.9% of creators do this poorly (or not at all). This book is a blueprint for better email that's more personal. Devour it."

—André Chaperon, sovereign world builder, creator, and writer

"Most marketers treat sending emails like fishing with dynamite. They throw copy in the inboxes of thousands, it explodes, and, for some reason, they hope that people happily buy their products after being treated that way.

Brennan will show you a much better way. He understands that long-term business success is built on fostering real and meaningful connections, and he has found the perfect framework to bring that to your business.

In a world where everyone sends the same messages to everyone, you will go far by engaging them as the real people they are. You'll write better emails and build a better business. This book will guide the way."

—Arvid Kahl, author and serial entrepreneur

"*This Is Personal* is a mandatory read for anyone in business today. Automation and machine learning seem to be dominating the spotlight while the importance of human connection is being forgotten. Brennan nails exactly how to approach marketing the right way."

—Pat Flynn, Founder of SPI Media

"Brennan Dunn is a veritable Nostradamus of digital marketing. *This Is Personal* leaves no stone unturned in the conversation around the future of email. Not only does this book include actionable strategies and a wealth of real-world examples, it also takes the jargony abstract concept of segmentation and breaks it down beautifully for the average business owner.

Why does that matter? Because segmentation, a.k.a. making marketing *personal*, is the most underutilized yet powerful revenue boosting strategy available to online business owners today. Your time is precious; this book is worth it."

—Chanti Zak, Quiz Funnel Strategist and Copywriter

"Buy this book right now. Any single chapter makes it worth it. I love Brennan's approach to Shadow Newsletters, which makes so much sense you wonder why you never thought of it before. Throughout the book, it's the simple and straightforward explanations (like the explanation of Immersion Sequences) that makes you feel like Brennan isn't just explaining things but cheering you on."

—Chris Lema, CEO of Motivations AI

"Brennan is a true master at personalization and email marketing. I've been following him since 2013 and am consistently blown away by how well-crafted and underrated his work is.

This book is no different. Brennan gives you the blueprint to implement everything he's learned in an easy-to-follow process.

These aren't growth hacks or fly-by-night tactics. His system is a timeless, evergreen approach that anyone can learn from.

If you're looking to grow an engaged audience and build a base of raving fans, this is a must-read."

—Chenell Basilio, writer and "Reverse Engineer"

THIS
IS
PERSONAL

THIS
IS
PERSONAL

The Art of Delivering the Right Email at the Right Time

BRENNAN DUNN

Matt Holt Books
An Imprint of BenBella Books, Inc.
Dallas, TX

Matt Holt is an imprint of BenBella Books, Inc.
10440 N. Central Expressway
Suite 800
Dallas, TX 75231
benbellabooks.com
Send feedback to feedback@benbellabooks.com

BenBella and *Matt Holt* are federally registered trademarks.

Printed in the United States of America
10 9 8 7 6 5 4 3 2 1

Library of Congress Control Number: 2023008411
ISBN 9781637742006 (hardcover)
ISBN 9781637742013 (electronic)

Editing by Gregory Newton Brown
Copyediting by Michael Fedison
Proofreading by Becky Maines and Cape Cod Compositors, Inc.
Indexing by Amy Murphy
Text design and composition by PerfecType, Nashville, TN
Cover design by Brigid Pearson
Emoji by Neo / stock.adobe.com
Printed by Lake Book Manufacturing

*To Laura, who proved once again that she's willing
to suffer through every endeavor I undertake.*

Contents

Introduction

THINGS ARE EASIER OFFLINE

THE DEATH OF THE HIGH STREET

I live in a small market town in the middle of England, and our high street (what my former self would have called "Main Street") is pretty run-down. There are a handful of cafés, some charity shops, and a bunch of hair salons. But, for the most part, most are in agreement that the glory days of the British high street and the American main street are long gone.

The culprit? Online shopping. The internet. And, more recently, COVID and lockdowns.

Ask most people why the internet has killed shopping malls and high streets and the answer is usually related to convenience. After all, you can find what you want online, click a few buttons, plug in your credit card, and a few days later a courier drops it off at your house. These days, you can even minimize both button clicking and waiting with the likes of Amazon: find what you want, click a buy button (they already have your credit card and address on file), and in just a few hours you might have what you need.

The pace of innovation online has continued at runaway speed, spilling over into other industries. Pop-up restaurants without a proper storefront, when paired with a food delivery service like Just Eat, are allowing upstart restaurateurs to pilot new ventures and make a bunch of money in the process, sidestepping the muck involved in starting up a new brick-and-mortar restaurant. Taxi companies, with their expensive medallion licensing process, have been struggling against the likes of Uber, which lets anyone with a car deliver the same result.

The unsung hero of this whole transition has been the introduction of personalized marketing, which is also the focus of the book before you. Giants like Amazon aren't hammering the same marketing messages to their entire customer database. Instead, they have a sophisticated machine learning operation that allows them to look at what *you're* looking at and what *you're* buying, and then model a profile that's specific to you. After that, they automatically create email messages that promote products *you'd* like to your inbox, and they probably reinforce these same products through banner and news feed ads.

This level of personalization has never been possible before. The closest parallel is walking into a shop and being greeted by the shopkeeper who knows you by name, recalls what you've bought from him before, and remembers to ask about your kids. But this just isn't possible when you have a customer base of 150 million (the number of Amazon Prime subscribers, as of March 2021).

What Amazon and others have capitalized on is the simple fact that customers want to be treated like people. While we've happily survived and thrived in the outgoing world of broadcast mass media and marketing, it has always lacked the one thing that we crave as humans: personal connection. The unique nature of the internet, and especially email marketing, has enabled savvy businesses to find the middle ground, the via media, between your great-great-grandfather being treated as a regular by his tailor and the spray-and-pray mass marketing of yesteryear.

A TRANSACTIONAL NATURE

As humans, we're wired to pick up on context and clues. If you've ever tried to sell someone on anything—this could be a gadget at a retail shop or a marriage proposal to a longtime partner—then you know how important it is to find a way to make what you're pitching attractive and obvious to who you're pitching to. We do this by asking, listening, and observing. And we take what we pick up, make on-the-fly adjustments, and tweak what it is we're saying.

Since our early ancestors started trading with each other millennia ago, this is how we've interacted *and* transacted. I have something I want you to do (e.g., exchange *this* for *that*), and the best way for me to do that is to individually assess what's in it for you and make it obvious why you'd be nuts to pass up my offer. You could rightfully say that this is, quite literally, baked into our DNA.

Yet online, and in the world of "mass media," a different approach is required. A billboard designer can't tailor their message for each passing car, so a one-size-fits-all message is created. It's the job of a great copywriter to think, "How do I make what I have to say as appealing as possible for the sort of people we want as customers?" and to then turn whatever they come up with into a message or offer.

The earliest forms of advertising took the form of letters. These pioneering sales letters had a lot of "you"s in them, and they were written as if you were being spoken to individually by someone who knew you. Obviously, these letters—the majority of which were found in periodicals or newspapers—weren't written to *you* personally, but what mattered was that they *felt like* they were. That's why they were, and often still are, so effective.

But you can't fit a full letter in Times Square. Furthermore, letters aren't that catchy—they're information dense, and they don't lend themselves to pulling in someone from whatever it is they were doing to focus and read. So, in a shorter form, punchier advertising had to be figured out and dialed in. But with fewer words available, the job of the copywriter and the illustrator became even more critical. Interest had to be piqued, and people had to be convinced, all within a message that took up significantly less real estate than a long-form sales letter. Without the benefit of being reactive and adaptive, the message had to be tailored differently to each individual as well.

For the last hundred or so years, this is how advertising has worked. Mass media marketing—billboards, radio jingles, television adverts, and the like—have become the de facto way for brands to introduce themselves to us, and for brands to pitch us on what they have to offer. You likely became familiar with a brand like Coca-Cola because it was everywhere . . . literally. You'd hear about it in your car. You'd see their vending machines. And a new ad involving cute polar bears would show up every Christmas.

The world of mass media marketing has also been paired with the rise of department stores. Your great-great-grandfather would have ordered his clothing from a tailor, while your great-great-grandmother would have turned to the dressmaker. They weren't buying from brands; they were buying something custom and made-to-measure from their local clothes maker.

But then something changed. Enter the likes of Sears, Roebuck & Co., and suddenly clothes, along with everything else (including houses!), were sold from a catalog or in-store. People would browse, look around, and compare. Brands emerged and began to seriously pitch themselves against their competition. No longer did a customer just pop into their local tailor and get measured for a suit jacket. Rather, they'd find their next jacket by flipping through a Sears catalog. The rise of ready-to-wear fashion coincided with the rise of packaged advertising.

For most of us, this is the world we grew up with. We'd drive to the mall, browse through shops, and buy. Whatever brands did the best job at getting their broadcast messages in front of us would probably get our business. But we rarely interacted with the brands directly—we'd buy from a shop like Macy's, who would be reselling the pair of Levi's jeans we wanted. This was a messy, noisy, one-size-fits-all method of getting customers. Now the internet has totally turned the whole model on its head, leading to a *lot* of empty, dying shopping malls (and small American and English downtowns).

INTRODUCING THIS IS PERSONAL

I'd like to introduce you to a framework for individually connecting with customers at exactly the right time and in exactly the right way. The This Is Personal framework is one that you can use for your business, *regardless* of what you're selling and who you're selling to, to create more personal connections with your customers over email.

While you're not going to be able to invest the thousands of engineers that Amazon has at putting together the perfect personalization platform, you'll be able to leverage off-the-shelf tools (that you're probably already paying for!) to find out who you're serving, what they uniquely want from you, and then tailor what you have to speak directly to them.

Together, we'll create the beginnings of this framework using this book as your guide. And even if you're running your business solo, are insanely busy, and don't identify as a "marketer," I'll guide you step-by-step through the measures you can take to build an online audience; individually find out who they are and what they want from you; and craft a plan for showing them what you've got, who you are, and why they should buy from you. This seems daunting, but it really isn't. As with most things related to your business, this will be a work in progress. You'll start small and simply, by getting some results and data, and then build from there.

The framework consists of nine components. I'll run through each here. Chapter one will contextualize the whys and hows of email. Then, in the remainder of the book, we'll explore each element of the framework in depth, chapter by chapter.

Component One: Positioning Your Marketing for Better Alignment

Anytime you've ever tried to sell anyone on anything, you've had to position your product or service against the need a would-be customer has.

There's a lot of talk on positioning—especially as it relates to pointing your business toward a specific type of customer who has a specific type of need—but much of it ends up overly academic and pretty difficult to not only figure out but, most importantly, to do anything with. This book takes a pretty simplistic, but ridiculously powerful, approach to positioning: it's just alignment.

In the late 2000s, I ran a small web agency. My job, as the owner, was to keep the team busy; therefore, my days were spent trying to get companies to hire us. As a "product" we could do a lot of things for a lot of different use cases. Our ability to write code and design web pages could be applied to just about every domain.

So when it came to writing a proposal, which was more or less a sales letter for one (the intended client), I had to determine how to best take our product—coding and web design—and align it to the specific and unique need of the client. While the raw materials—my team and their time—were always the same across our projects, how I went about describing the reason for writing code or crafting designs would change. I had to align our team with a particular project. The end result, the proposal, was our offer.

When I think about positioning, it's just this. It's aligning a need with a product. The mistake I think too many people make is thinking that you need to radically transform your entire business model and go all in on a particular position.

In the following chapters, we'll look at why this doesn't need to be the case, and why you can instead change how you describe what you're selling and why it matters depending on who's listening.

OUTCOME

Substantially higher conversions and sales because you're able to highlight "what's in it for me?" for each person. When you cast a wide net, which is how most people typically pitch online, you put the onus on the buyer to figure out how what you're saying specifically applies to their situation.

Component Two: Utilizing the Power of Segmentation

In order to dynamically position your offers, you first need to have the underlying data that will help you decide how to best pitch someone. You'll do this by segmenting your email list based on two primary dimensions: *who* somebody is and *what* they're currently struggling with. This data will then allow you to deliver highly targeted messages, sending the right messages to exactly the right people.

In this chapter, you'll learn how to incorporate feedback loops and progressive profiling methods that allow you to always learn more about your audience. What you learn will end up neatly filed in your email marketing database, and you'll be able to learn a lot more about everyone on your email list.

OUTCOME

An in-depth, data-backed understanding of the composition of your audience. It's straightforward enough to use insight tools from publishers like YouTube or Google Analytics to know location, gender, age approximation, and other bits of demographic data—but by collecting zero-party data about your audience, you'll know what people are struggling with, how they self-identify, and other information that'll help you deliver highly personalized messages.

Component Three: Building Your Audience

Now that you understand the power of personalized messaging, and the necessity to have segmentation data that informs personalization, you'll learn how to create a new system for growing your online audience or enhancing the ones you already have in place.

This chapter's all about how to get "drive-by," anonymous visitors to opt in to hearing more from you, and to eventually be sold to by you. The online landscape is full of lead magnets and opt-in forms that try to turn casual web searches, intriguing social shares, and more into your latest subscriber, but these lead generation forms are almost always one-size-fits-all: everyone sees the same form, the same opt-in offer, the same calls to action.

Using what you now know about how to personalize your messaging using zero-party data (data voluntarily given by consumers), you'll learn how to start thinking, "Why would *this person* want to hear more from us?"

OUTCOME

More people joining your email list, which means more potential future customers and brand advocates. You'll not only be collecting basic information like someone's first name and email address, but will also have a pretty solid understanding of what they're looking for from your brand and who they are (e.g., the industry they work in, their job role, their fitness level).

Component Four: Rolling Out the Welcome Mat

Many brands now begin new relationships over email with a "welcome sequence." This is preferred to just throwing whatever live broadcast or newsletter content you have at someone. After all, it can be a bit disorienting to get hit with a launch promotion or end up knee-deep in a multipart email newsletter series a few days after joining a list.

You'll learn how to formulate and create highly personal, interactive welcome sequences that take into account the segmentation data you have about your new subscriber. This will allow you to break away from a canned series of emails that say the same thing to everyone, in favor of a sequence that greets someone given what you know about them, and addresses that you're listening and plan to give them exactly what they're looking for—and nothing else.

OUTCOME

Lackluster welcome sequences usually lead to people getting turned off of a brand fairly quickly. Either they're too outright promotional, or they're just tone-deaf to the underlying needs of the new subscriber. Each new subscriber relationship will start with someone who's eager to hear more from you because you've made it clear that you empathize with who they are and have a plan for helping them with what they need.

Component Five: Creating Customers

Armed with knowledge about each new subscriber, you can now get to work curating personalized "customer creation" sequences. The idea is simple: not everyone who comes across your brand knows that they need what you offer. As a result, brands will bombard their email list with marketing emails, but not everyone on the receiving end is ready to be pitched. They sometimes don't know they suffer from the problem your product purports to solve, *or* they are aware of the problem but don't think it's troublesome enough to do anything about it right now. Creating customers is all about meeting your new subscribers where they are today, demonstrating empathy using the data you have about them, and then leading them to understand the gravity of the problem, the solvability of the problem, and your recommendations for helping them get rid of it once and for all. The end result is someone who knows they need help and can now be fully receptive to whatever offers you have to help them solve said problem.

OUTCOME

A crash course into the problem space that your brand operates in. This will be an educational sequence that's designed to get someone on your wavelength. It will "set the stage" and give someone the foundational understanding they need to truly understand why they need something like what you offer. The automation you create will then pitch someone on how you can help them once they're sufficiently prepared.

Component Six: Making the Perfect Pitch

Once you know a bit about who someone is—namely a little about what they're looking for from you, along with how they see the world—you're then able to craft a succinct and obvious reason for them to do business with you.

You'll learn how to not only set up and structure compelling email pitches, but also how to leverage the segmentation data you'll be sitting on to deliver the perfect pitch.

OUTCOME

Many, many more sales. More relevant messaging leads to more people reading what you have to say. And that leads to more people hearing about what you have to offer them. And this increased engagement leads ultimately to more sales.

Component Seven: Playing the Long Game

Between your promotions, you're going to need to keep your list "warm" and engaged. To effectively sell over email, you need to both continuously educate and continuously sell. Focus too much time on just education, and your sales will suffer. Focus too much on selling? Your engagement will drop, your list will tire, and . . . sales will suffer.

Here you'll learn how to keep your list engaged, and how to send long-term nurturing content that not only continues to prepare people to become customers, but also gets your subscribers to become brand advocates.

OUTCOME

Higher retention and engagement, and the license you need to continue to promote your products and services. You'll also see how to amplify list growth by creating a referral program and learn how to automate your long-term nurturing.

Component Eight: Building in the Open

Your email list can be one of the most valuable business assets you own. Besides a willing audience of buyers, your list can also be used to run your own market and product research campaigns.

You'll see how you can use your email list to pioneer new product ideas and build excitement for future products or services you're working on.

OUTCOME

An invaluable resource for piloting new projects, a captive audience of ready-to-buy customers, and so much more.

Component Nine: Understanding the New Role of Social Media

This is a book about email, but I'm not so much of a curmudgeon that I think social media has no use. It's actually extremely useful, especially when used to build your audience and channel people toward the email system you've set up.

You'll learn a few creative ways of using social media to build your business, like how to use Twitter and LinkedIn to tease out ideas that you might have included in your emails, and then pitch people on the idea of joining your automation sequences—and *not* just pitching your products or services outright.

OUTCOME

A new approach to using social media to build your email audience, along with some ideas around getting your readers and customers to engage with your brand.

First, as I mentioned above, we'll start our journey by figuring out what email really is, why it works, and how to best make it matter for you and your company.

Chapter 1

CUSTOMERS ARE PEOPLE, TOO

HOW DOES EMAIL WORK?

When I first got online as a kid, AOL Instant Messenger (AIM) was the de facto way to communicate for those of us fortunate enough to have access to the internet.

But AIM is long gone (it was officially shut down in 2017).

Since AIM, a number of other instant messaging services have come and gone. ICQ, MSN Messenger, Yahoo! Messenger, Google Hangouts, and more are either technically mothballed or have fizzled into obscurity.

Depending on when you're reading this book, instant messaging (or "direct messaging") will absolutely still be around—but the platform you use to message someone might be quite a bit different from the major platforms available at the time of writing.

People, especially those with skin in the emerging marketing technology game, have long been predicting the same fate for email.

Email is *old* tech. In 1971—more than fifty years ago—the first email was sent from one user in a shared system to another user. This is where the at-notation (@) format came from, and it is still used to this day. Every email address includes two bits of key information—the user and the system, or domain: "john.doe" at the "Gmail" system.

Not much has really changed with email since the '70s. When an email is sent, the following happens:

- A Simple Mail Transfer Protocol server (SMTP) gets a copy of the email, which is made up of a sender, recipient(s), a subject, and the body—or content—of the message.
- The SMTP server's job is to take a copy of that message and send it to all the various recipients it should go to. If it's just one recipient, this is relatively straightforward. The IP address (think: internet street address) of the domain name (@gmail. com) is figured out. Then the SMTP knocks on Gmail's proverbial door and says, "Hey, I have a message for john.doe."
- The receiving mail server over at Gmail can either accept the message or tell the SMTP server that "john.doe" doesn't live here, or hasn't paid rent lately, or has no room for any more emails. The latter examples are all known as "bounces."
- If the mail server does agree to receive the incoming message, it makes a complete copy of the incoming email and places it in the target account's inbox.
- John Doe, assuming he has push notifications enabled on his phone, might then see that he has a new email.

If there are multiple recipients, then the above takes place quite a few times. Each exchange is atomic: "Does this user have an inbox on your system? And will you accept this message? Okay, here's the message. Thank you, goodbye." These exchanges are also irreversible—once an email is delivered, it's delivered. The sender's SMTP server has no knowledge beyond what the receiving mail server has said. Does the recipient open the email? Read half of it? Read it all? Download the attachments? None of that information is passed back by the receiving mail server.

Over the decades, marketers and technology companies have tried to improve upon the email protocol's simplicity. After all, if we can delete Facebook posts—why can't we delete emails we've sent? Companies like Microsoft have tried to implement handshake agreements of sorts for things like deleting already-sent emails. If an email is sent from one Outlook account to another, the sending Outlook account can decide to try to "unsend" that message. Any other Outlook inboxes that received that message can pick up on that request and then forcefully yank it out of the recipient's inbox.

The above isn't a feature of email—rather it's an optimization layer that email servers and email clients are free to ignore. Outlook might be able to *ask* to have an email taken away, but once it's out of the gate (the SMTP server), it's gone. Remember, every email that ends up in your inbox is a *copy* of the original.

Additionally, marketers have never really liked that email as a protocol doesn't have any built-in mechanism for letting senders know if their email has been engaged with. To circumvent this limitation, they started including "tracking pixels" in their emails. These are invisible images that are loaded alongside any other pictures that might end up in an email. But these images aren't actually included *in* the content of the email itself—rather, they're loaded off a remote server. An analytics server, actually. When an email client tries to load this pseudo-image, the URL being loaded includes the email address of the recipient. And since the *only* way for this URL to ever be accessed is for someone to open an email and attempt to load the images inside, this allows that analytics server to then say, "Aha! john. doe@gmail.com has just opened the 'Check out our latest sale' email."

The same thing has been done to track clicks. If you send out a marketing email that's supposed to link to https://yoursite.com/new-product, your email marketing software is going to translate that to point instead to their servers. When one of your reader's clicks that link—thinking they're going to your website—they're first brought to your email marketing software's server, which logs a click, before they're forwarded on to your website. Unless the reader is super savvy, they probably have no idea that this middleman even exists.

These examples—deleting sent emails, tracking email opens, tracking clicks—are all creative work-arounds to the simple messaging platform that is email. Because they're work-arounds, they'll often fail. For example, if a user of Outlook sends someone an email who uses iCloud (Apple's email service), they're not going to be able to "unsend" that email because Apple hasn't implemented that functionality into their email client. Gmail optimistically blocks opening images from dubious senders, which means that unless the recipient clicks "Display images," the sender won't have any idea the email was read—even if it was. And, as of recently, Apple's built-in email client preloads *all* email, including their tracking pixels, by default.

These days, if you post something on Twitter, you can see detailed stats about how many people saw it, how many engaged with it, clicked it, and so on. This is all possible because Twitter controls the medium. They hold all the keys. They built the technology. Your tweets and my tweets all happily coexist in the exact same database.

This also means that companies like Twitter can innovate in a way that email, as an "ownerless," decentralized platform, can't. Before November of 2009, there was no way to actually retweet anything on Twitter. Users instead would prepend "RT" to tweets they wanted to promote to their followers. Since Twitter owned the platform, they could simply build a retweet feature, which is exactly what they did.

When marketers say they want email to die and be replaced with something else, it's largely due to the above-mentioned limitations. Email just doesn't change. And emails are displayed in lots of different email clients, which has meant that how emails are *designed*—the HTML code that powers the emails you see in your inbox—has stagnated. In fact, if you want to reliably send an email that should look good everywhere, you need to design it using the exact same web design technologies that were state of the art in the late 1990s.

These limitations, however, are also advantages. And I'm glad that email hasn't been successfully killed off. Its simplicity and pervasiveness mean that I, as a marketer, can do things that just aren't possible on other communications platforms, like Facebook or Twitter.

Let's look at what these things are.

SIX REASONS I THINK YOU SHOULD GO ALL IN ON EMAIL (EVEN THOUGH IT'S OLD)

This is a book about email and why you should use it.

I'm obviously going to be a bit biased. But with the stage now set, I want to try to convince you (if I need to!) that you should be focused on email for growth and sales, despite the siren's call of the social media platform du jour.

1. *Email Is* Relational

Email is relational, and more than in a "Hi FIRST_NAME" sort of way.

When you tweet something publicly, everyone who follows you (or looks at your profile) can see it.

There's no way for me to just say, "Send this tweet about this cool email marketing thing I did just to my followers who care about email marketing."

You can do that with email, however—assuming you're segmenting your list correctly.

Different messages, different tones, different examples, and entirely different campaigns can be used depending on what you know about the people on the receiving end.

The only real way to accomplish something like that on a firehose platform like social media is to create separate channels or accounts, like what Linus Tech Tips has done with their "Mac Address" YouTube channel, designed for the segment of their viewership who also use Apple products.[1]

2. *Email Allows for* Life-Cycle Messaging

Email automation can be used to send messages to people based on where they are in your funnel/journey/awareness-of-whatever-it-is-you've-got-going-on.

Someone new to your email list can be gently introduced to your brand and why you do what you do, slowly becoming acclimated to the worldview you hold and the products you offer.

Likewise, when someone ends up becoming super engaged (using whatever set of metrics you use to determine that) or achieves a milestone, like becoming a customer or reading your newsletters for three months, you can then do things like asking people to become affiliates, refer you, or send you a testimonial.

With social media, you can't really do this. *All* of your followers are privy to whatever you happen to be posting at the time, regardless of whether it's the "right" time for them to hear what you have to say.

3. *Email Is* Permanent

When I'm at a conference, either as a speaker or an attendee, I'm *at* the conference. I don't check my email. And I only go on social media if I want to share a takeaway from a talk I'm watching, or as a cheeky attempt to game the conference hashtag and get more people to attend my talk. I try my best to stay present and be a part of the impromptu community as much as I'm able to.

Over the last few months, I've presented a new talk on email marketing at a few conferences. During the presentation, I always comment about how I'll be returning home to a runaway inbox . . . and that any and all tweets or Facebook posts or Instagram stories that were shared during the conference will probably never be seen by me.

This is because email is permanent. It needs to be acted on. You get an email, and you either read it and archive or outright delete it. It hangs out in your inbox until one of those things happens. On the other hand, social media is ephemeral. While you can absolutely scroll back through someone's Facebook posts, the nature of the algorithm means that the *newest* stuff from people you follow will always be prioritized.

For better or worse, you need to act on every email you get. Or simply declare email bankruptcy and end up with tens of thousands of unread emails.

4. Email Is Universal

The people you most likely want to do business with have an email account. Signing up for virtually anything online requires one. Even when you decide to sign up for a service using your Facebook or Apple account, the service you sign up for still pulls your email address and associates it with the single-click sign-on account you used. After all, when they send you an invoice, they're not going to send it as a Facebook message—it's an email.

According to a report put out by 99firms, more than 50 percent of the world's population uses email, 90 percent of Americans over fifteen years old use it, and 96 percent of consumers check their email daily.[2] No social media platform can get anywhere close to these numbers.

5. Email Is Decentralized

Earlier I explained that no one "owns" email. Email is truly portable, especially if you own your own domain name. If I get fed up with Gmail, I can move to Fastmail. The people who email you won't need to know that you've changed anything, because the address they're sending to remains the same.

The fact that no one owns email is one of its best attributes. You never need to worry about anyone prioritizing some emails ahead of others. And, sure, this means that email spammers will never go away. But this also means that no one company can "update the algorithm" and derail your entire email marketing strategy overnight.

6. *Email Is* Flexible

And, finally, email allows for unparalleled flexibility. When you send a bulk email campaign to thousands of people, the email platform that's doing the sending is still generating *individual* emails. Even if you do no personalization whatsoever, a campaign sent to one thousand people gets one thousand unique email "objects" created and sent.

But when introducing personalization into your emails, whether that's adding someone's name to the beginning of a message or reshaping the entire flow and feel of a message based on subscriber segmentation data, the email platform you use is up for the challenge. Modern email platforms have built-in personalization tools that enable you to truly customize each message and make it individually relevant to each recipient. Doing this, however, requires some segmentation data—and you'll learn how to capture that data in a few chapters.

Chapter 2

POSITION YOUR MARKETING, NOT YOUR OFFERINGS

Life is a series of transactions.

In school, I used to attempt to get better snacks from friends than the ones my mom sent along with me. This involved figuring out who was gullible enough to value crackers more than, say, their pack of Gushers. I wasn't deviant or malicious—I just knew what I liked. And at that age, it wasn't a small bag of Ritz crackers.

To successfully barter crackers for Gushers, I needed to try to convince someone to transact with me. Your Gushers, my crackers. In my own grade school way, this required me to figure out *why* someone should perceive their snack as inferior and mine as superior. And given my offering (crackers), this was usually a tough sell.

But selling is exactly what it was. And it's really not far off from all the other major and minor transactions I've been involved with since then.

A big part of being a fully functioning member of society is learning how to transact. You could probably go as far as to say it's the foundation of our civilization. Deciding who to marry, and then getting them to agree to it, is a pretty major transaction. As is buying a house, selling an employer on hiring you, and making your first dollar on the internet.

So what does any of this have to do with positioning?

Well, in order for a transaction to go ahead, two parties first need to agree on it: here's where two parties come into "alignment." As the person who wants to get hired at a company, you need to sell yourself to be appealing to the employer. They're not going to transact with you (that is, offer you a desk and a fortnightly salary) without first deciding that you're likely offering something that outweighs the salary they'll pay you. To do this, a smart interviewee does a bit of homework first: Who is this company? What does it sell? How large is it? When did it start? Who's hiring me? What's their role at the company? How long does LinkedIn say they've been with the company? And so on.

All of that data will then end up being used by the interviewee to make themselves even more desirable—a "surer bet," if you will. This manifests in such ways as including examples of what you've done professionally that's closely aligned with what they do as a company. It might also mean providing a few seemingly off-the-cuff ideas around how you could see yourself helping the company grow, given what you know about its current business. Or, more superficially, it could take the form of small talk around how you know so-and-so, who went to the interviewer's university.

The smart interviewee knows that the single best thing they can do is to align themselves perfectly with the needs of a business. The business has a role to fill, and they expect whoever fills that role to deliver something that creates more value for the business than they're paying out. For example, if they're budgeting $70,000 a year for a web designer, they're expecting the material work that that designer does—the ads, the website optimizations, the trade show banners—will far outweigh the cost. This is why most businesses pay for things, including people. They either want to make more revenue or find a way to reduce expenses. Both of which, of course, result in more profit.

If the smart interviewee knows this equation and tailors how they describe themselves and their value to perfectly fit what a company is looking for . . . why can't we do the same in our emails to potential customers? Why do we need to standardize on a one-size-fits-all way of describing our products and services? Why don't we do exactly what we do in the offline world and come up with a compelling reason that a specific type of person with a specific type of problem might want what we have?

THE DYNAMIC BUSINESS

Sales-first organizations are pretty great at this. Their sales team is well versed on how their products have been applied across any number of industries. They know what particular benefits appeal to different types of decision makers. And they're going to be pretty adept at tailoring what they're selling, and possibly even how it's packaged (e.g., pricing, bundled components, and so on), accordingly.

But not all of us have a sales team. Many of us sell to a faceless, online audience who, independently of any individual prodding, decide (or don't decide) to enter their personal information and buy from us. Our customers only ever actually talk to us when something goes wrong; the normal customer journey has them discovering our products, deciding what products are right for them, and buying those products entirely without any individual human interaction.

Whether you consider yourself as a business-to-business or a business-to-consumer organization, you're ultimately selling to people. Full stop. And people are all wired pretty similarly. They're triggered to do things that they think will make them feel better, experience pleasure, or be regarded by the people who matter to them as a valiant hero.

These triggers are something we'll continue to come back to throughout this book, but here's a set of rubrics that I think make sense to internalize right away:

When selling to businesses:
- How can you help them *make more money?*
- How can you help them *spend less money?*
- . . . Both outcomes lead to more profit.

What do the individuals you're selling to at a business care about?
- *If it's the owner,* or the direct beneficiary of "more profit," it's exactly that—helping them inflate their lifestyle and their ego by making their business more efficient and putting more money in their pockets.
- *If it's an employee/department*—that is, someone whose pay isn't directly tied to the overall profits of a business—it's to make them shine. If it's because of them that their department's output is up 150 percent YTY, or because of them that increased online orders have led to opening a brand-new distribution center, that person or team become rock stars. And rock stars get rewarded, usually with promotions or pay raises.
- . . . Usually, it's all about more personal take-home money.

When selling to consumers:
- How can you help them feel like they matter more to others (more praise, more dates, more sex, more friends)?
- How can you help them feel more secure (more resources, a safer house, better at self-defense, better health and longevity)?
- How can you help them reach apotheosis (feeling fulfilled, feeling at one with themselves and the world around them, becoming the best version of themselves)?

Maslow's Hierarchy of Needs outlines our human needs quite nicely.

Ultimately, our monkey brains just want to survive. We want food and drink, shelter from the elements, and clothes on our back. Once we've secured that, we want to know that things will stay somewhat stable: we want security and some state of permanence. Beyond that, we need relationships. Humans *are* social creatures, after all. We want a companion, and we want friends. And generally we don't just want people around us: we want them to actually really like us—so the next rung of the hierarchy is the desire for prestige. And, finally, once we have our physical and political foundations in place, we next want to reach apotheosis—or self-actualization. We want to feel like we're leaving a legacy, that we're making some dent in this void of a universe we happen to inhabit.

As I show in Figure 1, when you're selling to businesses, you're ultimately trying to make the people who either own or work at the business be better off than they were before. This directly translates into them being materially *and personally* more secure, which reinforces the lower rungs of their personal hierarchy of needs.

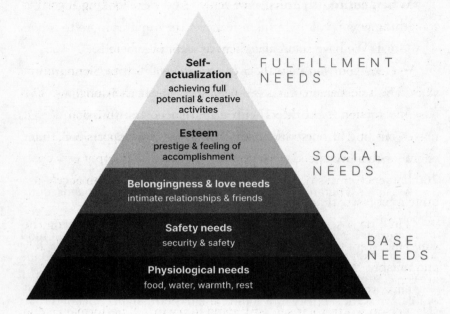

Figure 1

So, ultimately, no matter if you regard yourself as a B2B or a B2C business, you're selling to people, and they're buying so that the human animal in them can ultimately feel more stable and secure. That's it.

THE IMPORTANCE OF POSITIONING

Imagine that you, your partner, and a brood of small children—yours, of course—all converge on a Toyota dealership one sunny Saturday afternoon. You pull up in a knackered old minivan. You're easily spotted, and a smartly dressed salesperson briskly walks out of the lobby and greets you in the parking lot.

"Hello! How may I help you?" asks the overly friendly salesperson.

"Our van is on its last leg," you reply. "And we're looking at getting something new."

"Great! We have some new Siennas right over here . . ."

You and your family walk over to a line of Toyota Sienna mini-vans. The salesperson starts telling you all about their engines. The baseline version is 3.0 liters with a four-speed transmission, and it maxes out at 210 horsepower. The XLE, however, sports a 3.3-liter engine with a five-speed transmission, and its power output gets up to 266 horsepower. It's quite a bit sportier and will be able to accelerate quite a bit faster than the baseline model—

"Hold on a second," you think. "I'm not planning on racing the van. I just want to get me and my family from Point A to Point B safely and reliably. What's this guy going on about?"

This would probably never happen in reality, because any car salesperson worth their salt isn't going to try to sell performance and speed to someone with their kids. But static businesses—the online sort where the same marketing campaigns are going out to everyone—typically have no idea if the recipient is looking for something safe, something fast, or something reliable. So they need to either go all in on one angle or find a way of diluting their messaging down to cover all the bases.

Kathy Sierra, author of the *Head First* series of programming books and *Badass: Making Users Awesome*, once told the story of a software consulting project that she and her team worked on for a major car manufacturer.[3]

The manufacturer wanted to install a series of kiosks throughout their showrooms that would serve to augment the sales team and also provide some exploratory entertainment for anyone stuck waiting for their car to be serviced.

The job of the kiosks was to help people see what various car models were available, what each one offered, and so on. What Kathy's team ended up building was pretty brilliant. Rather than launching someone into deciding on the type of car—i.e., a sedan, convertible, minivan, SUV, or whatever—the kiosk would first find out a bit more about you.

What's most important to you in a car?
- Safety
- Reliability/maintenance costs
- Resale value
- Performance

Depending on what you selected, the descriptions of the cars you'd look at would change . . . slightly. Here's how Kathy describes these changes: "For example, if the person said, 'I care about safety more than I care about maintenance costs,' then on the screen that talks about the engineering of the car, the headline would say something like, 'Engineered with your safety in mind . . .' or something like that. And we might throw in a gratuitous picture of a kid in a car seat. (Yeah, I *know* that's manipulative, but it wasn't untrue.)"

The brilliance of the project was that this wasn't some crazy complex or expensive undertaking. The manufacturer didn't have a large budget laid out to really personalize this kiosk experience all that much, but they obviously wanted to do whatever they could to keep more people using it.

"The main point of the system, though, was that 99 *percent of the content was the same for every user*," Kathy continued. "We didn't have custom-tailored screens other than the banner at the top. But it turned out that by orienting the content—the same content *everyone* saw—to something meaningful for that individual, the information became more relevant.

"Of course, you don't want to do this dishonestly—as it would be if we said something like, 'Your safety is our MOST IMPORTANT GOAL,' and then if you chose 'Resale value' we said, 'Maintaining your resale value is our MOST IMPORTANT GOAL.' But by putting a personally tailored headline over non-custom content, we were able to connect the content to the user's individual desires. Honest, but personalized.

"And, according to the client, it was a huge success! People spent much more time on each screen than in the previously uncustomized version."

The hypothetical salesperson who I described above—the one who randomly started going on about the engine, acceleration, and overall performance of the Sienna minivan—is probably a bit of a car geek. Numbers and such matter a lot to him. And that spilled over to his absurd attempt to sell someone with their family in tow on a van with information that just wasn't relevant or useful.

I want to close this example with another quote from Kathy's excellent article "Making Content Meaningful to Users":[4] "But the skilled and ethical salesperson, now they know that a potential user doesn't care about you as much as he cares about what this means for him. The good salesperson knows you don't care about technical details or even features. You care about what those features mean to you. *The good salesperson knows it isn't even about benefits, but about the benefits you care about.*"

Chapter 3

THE POWER OF SEGMENTATION

Anyone can put "Dear [First Name]," at the start of an email.
Nobody's fooled. It's still a stock form letter, blasted out to anyone
and everyone. What creates a sense of connection is a message that
takes the individual customer's needs into account. While no one
expects (or wants) to have their mind read, customers *do* expect you
to remember what you've learned about them: their buying history
and what they've chosen to share with you. Too many businesses
run surveys and then fail to act on answers that could meaningfully
improve the customer experience.

Imagine sharing your vacation plans with a colleague and, after
returning, discovering he'd forgotten where you'd been. Why ask if
you're not going to listen?

The key to using customer knowledge effectively is *segmentation,* which simply means organizing your audience according to their
needs, identities, and history with you. Done properly, segmentation
helps you direct your customers toward what they really want. It
requires collecting personal data, though, which presents a host of
legal, ethical, and logistical challenges. Controversies around social
media and privacy have made us all more wary about sharing our

data, regardless of whether it is sensitive (e.g., Social Security number) or simply personal (e.g., favorite color).

The solution to this quandary lies in asking the right questions. Good questions feel helpful, not intrusive. For example, I added a one-click survey to the sign-up form for an online golf retailer's website:

What's your swing speed?

I might have asked visitors to reveal their income level or to tally up how much they spend on golf equipment annually. But those are sterile, company-focused questions that are obviously meant to help the business, not the customer. They don't translate in any clear way into an improved customer experience.

In contrast, asking a simple question about swing speed isn't going to come across as prying or personal. We framed the question in terms of the customer's needs: "We'd love to point you toward the right drivers." In that context, asking about swing speed makes perfect sense because it's a good proxy for skill level: beginners and pros need different gear, and swing speed helps make that distinction. Any retail salesperson might ask the same thing.

Through the use of such simple on-site surveying, this website effectively reduced the signal-to-noise ratio for visitors. People found what they needed faster, with less digging and more certainty. In general, you don't want to add friction—additional form fields or other steps—when someone is submitting information to your site. In this case, however, asking a question actually boosted time on-site and led to a fourfold increase in email list sign-up rate.

Counterintuitively, the right questions *increase* engagement. That's because, as customers, we crave personalized information.

We're more than happy to answer questions *if* doing so will help us navigate the available options for the best outcome. We want the very best result *for us,* and good questions lead us to believe that the retailer can help us find it.

Asking good questions doesn't stop at sign-up. Customers start to relish the customized experience you can offer. Over time, they become eager to tell you more about themselves. They'll see that you're reacting to what you're learning about them in a very specific way, not just aggregating data for some PowerPoint slide. Over time, you can progressively hone your understanding of a customer's needs with feedback loops that course-correct their experience. This process is the foundation of a one-to-many way of communicating with customers that feels entirely one-to-one.

STAYING PERSONAL WITH 140,000+ EMAIL SUBSCRIBERS

Pat Flynn was getting his architectural career off the ground when an economic downturn got him laid off from his firm. With a wedding around the corner and family planning well under way, Pat decided to take his future into his own hands by starting an online business. He started blogging about "passive income" businesses online and, through grit and perseverance, built up a solid following. Today, Pat and his team run a healthy, seven-figure business called Smart Passive Income (SPI),[5] and they produce books, online courses, a popular podcast, and an annual conference.

Until recently, most of SPI's income came from affiliate marketing. They earned commissions by promoting third-party products on their own websites. Over the last few years, they've begun selling their own online courses, but the transition hasn't been easy. They have a big list, but when it comes to selling, there's more to a mailing list than its size.

In early 2018, Mindy Peters, the wizard behind Flynn's email empire, started surveying visitors to Smart Passive Income and organizing them into segments. Both on the website and over email, they'd ask a series of five questions starting with this one:

Which describes your business?
- I am just getting started (or thinking about starting a business).
- I have a business that makes $0–500/month.
- I have a business that makes more than $500/month.

This question touches on business income, which could certainly be seen as intrusive—if handled the wrong way—but the categories are too broad to offend all but the most privacy-sensitive visitors. SPI's website is focused on helping online businesses, so a little context around the question—*I want to give you exactly what you need to take that next step, nothing more*—made it palatable for his audience. Completion rates for all five questions were very high.

Within eight months, SPI had collected more than sixty thousand responses, each of which was automatically attached to the contact record of the email subscriber who had answered it. The remaining four questions—such as "Do you have a podcast?"—helped tailor their marketing, but this first one determined the overall segmentation of the list. The needs and preferences of an aspiring entrepreneur are very different from those of an active business owner already generating thousands of dollars in revenue a month. That distinction superseded all the rest.

SPI began using these three main segments to tailor the experience of all visitors. The headline shown to aspiring entrepreneurs read: "Let me help you build a passive income–driven online business." For those already making a few hundred dollars a month, it read: "Let me help you grow your online business with passive income." Those making even more revenue saw: "Let me teach you proven strategies to optimize your business." Crucially, SPI did not design three entirely different homepages. Most of the site functioned identically no matter who you were. Personalization allowed SPI to modify content only where necessary in order to speak to customers precisely where they are in their own entrepreneurial journeys. And that doesn't stop with headlines and welcome messages.

For Cyber Monday, the annual online marketing event that takes place after Thanksgiving, SPI ran their first personalized promotion. They had three courses available for sale and one more to presell. The question they now faced was how to leverage the list more effectively. In a blog post summarizing the campaign—the sort of hands-on content his audience loves—Pat wrote:

> As my team and I were discussing how to market all of these courses at the same time during a 48-hour sale period, it quickly became apparent that it could become very confusing (and potentially overwhelming) with all of the different products that were being offered at the same time.
>
> Too many options often [leads to] too little action.

Pat created a central landing page for incoming traffic during the promotion. But what to put there? He explained his reasoning:

> If you're building audiences and serving them with quality products, you want to be more direct when possible: "Have this specific problem? Here's this specific solution."
>
> Understanding who is in your audience and segmenting them based on the problems they might have and the language they specifically use is a significant advantage.

Segmenting by skill or experience alone wouldn't suffice. For example, Pat wanted to hide courses from people who had already purchased them. Marketing to someone who has already purchased a product is the kind of klutzy behavior that can make brand messaging feel so impersonal. As customers, we expect companies to know what we've purchased from them and take that into account when they talk to us. It's aggravating to be pitched on a product we've already bought—*especially* if it's on sale for less than what we paid! Much to the chagrin of privacy hawks, Target's algorithms are said to be sophisticated enough to predict a customer's need for diapers before they've discovered they're pregnant. Knowing that someone already bought a crib is table stakes next to that. Get it right!

Although SPI had three segments, they ended up creating eight versions of the basic sales page once the rest of the data had been taken into account. Each featured slight but useful variations in copy and product offerings. There is no shortcut for this kind of customization. Doing it properly means thinking through the needs and priorities of each segment instead of focusing on how much stuff you want to sell. (Technology aside, what kind of thinking could be more valuable for an entrepreneur?)

In short, it took a lot of work. Was it worth it? Let's see how the Cyber Monday promotion performed. In his post, Pat waxed rhapsodic:

> As a result of the campaign . . . we were able to increase revenue by $104,000. We discovered, through A/B testing against a control (which was the standard sales page), that [personalizing the sales page] helped us increase conversions by 2.38x. That means without it, we would have generated only $75,900 on our own.
>
> HOME RUN!
>
> That's a huge increase in income due to personalization. On one hand, I know I've built a ton of trust with my audience and would have likely done very well without [personalizing], but the numbers are that much higher that, even if the numbers aren't exactly correct here in the reporting, you can't deny that this is helping out, big time!

Of course, knowing that personalization works only goes so far. *How* did Pat, Mindy, and the team actually translate all of the data they'd collected about their customers into a simple, actionable, and effective plan? Why eight variations and not six, or twelve? Where do you even begin?

You may know your customers well, particularly if you've been in business for a while. You may even have a clear sense, on a macro level, of who they are and what they want from you. But segmentation makes this knowledge *specific*, *actionable*, and *effective*. Even a simple segmentation strategy will translate into more opt-ins to your list and more subscribers becoming customers. It's magical to see it in action.

Note the word "simple." There is no limit to the degree of sophistication you can employ with these techniques. In fact, one of the biggest concerns I hear from entrepreneurs considering this approach is its complexity. But you can't run until you can walk. Any business will see benefits by creating two segments to start. You need to know *whom* you serve and *why* they're coming to you.

WHO

Understanding your audience is essential for several reasons. One of the most underappreciated is that you learn how to talk to them. Nothing builds trust faster than speaking to your customers using their own words. For example, you need to know *who* they are, how they describe themselves. Hospitals serve "patients," law firms serve "clients," and retail stores serve "customers." All these terms describe "the people who keep you in business," but if your customers are lawyers and you call them "patients," they're going to worry. If you don't even grasp their lingo at such a basic level, what are the chances you're going to understand the specific problems they face? Safer to go with a company that really knows the category.

Naming things properly is just the beginning of establishing your credibility, of course. Learning more about your customers will affect all the language you use: in emails, on your website, and in any case studies, testimonials, and other social proof you use to convey the quality and relevance of your offering. Prospective customers want to see that others *like them* rely on your product or service. You can't convey that without knowing who they are first.

When setting up a segmentation strategy, companies often default to obvious characteristics like gender, age, and location.

Unless you plan on using that data in a meaningful way, there is no point in collecting any of it. Advice on weight loss or parenting *might* be tailored based on the customer's gender, but project management software certainly won't. Think it through. What information will actually help you show your customers that you understand them? To effectively sell project management software without a salesperson, you might need to know the person's industry, the size of their company, and maybe their role within the organization. If they run a marketing department, for example, you could highlight the specific benefits marketers care about, or display a case study of your software being used to launch a major marketing campaign. Technical leads, on the other hand, would care about things like security and uptime, and might be put off by a wall of endorsements from marketers.

Age? Location? Why ask questions like these if they won't improve the customer's experience or your sales process? By collecting this data, you're clouding your results with noise. You're also wasting the customer's time, and, worse, letting them see that you're wasting it. Everyone is familiar with these kinds of default questions, included on your form simply because they're included on everyone's form.

You're not the U.S. Census Bureau. Before you ask a single question, develop a plan for how you'll use every bit of data to make the customer's interactions with your site more useful. Unless an answer will help you speak to someone more effectively, don't ask the question. If you end up needing to know something else down the road, you can always go back and re-survey your list with a clear reasoning behind the new question. If it's something that will benefit your customers, they will be more than happy to tell you. After all, they're here to be served.

WHY

The other key piece of segmentation data is what the customer needs from you, their *why*. What keeps them on your mailing list or brings them to your site? Why are they here?

Figuring out the why can be much trickier than the who. Most businesses have only a vague sense of the reasons their customers choose them over the competition, or even why they want the product or service in the first place. You could make some informed guesses and collect data around those, cleverly excavating the truth. But it's much easier to just ask people. This can be as simple as sending an email to your entire list:

> Hi there! We want to be 100 percent positive that we're giving you exactly what you need from us.
>
> If you have a minute to spare, please reply to this email with one to two sentences describing who you are, what kind of business you run, and the number-one thing you're hoping to get help with from us.

If you don't yet have a meaningful email list, pick up the phone and call a few customers and leads. Chat with customers who come into your shop: Why'd they come in today, and what perception—if any—did they have about your business beforehand? This is appropriate whether you're a small-business lawyer, the owner of an art-supply shop, or a manager at a huge B2B service operation. If you position the call as an honest attempt to serve them better in the future, you'll be surprised how many are willing to open up. People want brands that *get* them. Asking these questions demonstrates that you're listening and that you're interested in staying personal as you continue to grow your business.

Gathering data in this way serves three functions. First, it helps you segment your audience. Second, it demonstrates your willingness to adapt in order to better serve your customers. Third, it provides that "voice-of-the-customer" language you'll use in the future to customize your communication. As discussed earlier, nothing builds trust like speaking to customers in their own words. Once you've created segments that usefully distinguish your key customer types, you can go back to the emails themselves to zero in on the words they use to describe themselves, their businesses, what they do, whom they serve, and the problems they face. You can use that same language to personalize pitches or sales pages directed to those segments.

Again, this is something that anyone would do instinctively when speaking face-to-face with a customer. It's how people build rapport. We're just using technology to make it work at scale.

TURNING ANSWERS INTO SEGMENTS

If you were a sales manager, you'd probably spend a good amount of time training your team on who the customer is. You'd combine quantitative sales data with qualitative experience to come up with a few core personas, or types of buyers.

Your website and email list are on your sales team, too. In fact, they work 24/7 and only occasionally call in sick. To get the most out of these workhorses, you need to train them using the data you collect by asking questions. To do this, you have to distill the mountain of raw feedback you've assembled into something that makes sense to a computer and can be used as the basis of your segmentation strategy.

45

This is easier to do than you might think, and it might be one of the most useful customer-discovery exercises you've ever done. You're going to use a simple spreadsheet. This spreadsheet is going to track and categorize the responses you've collected, allowing you to develop your initial segmentation strategy.

To start, create a new spreadsheet with two tabs: one for your primary *who* segments, the other for your primary *why* segments. Next, go through the data you've collected so far, one response at a time. Your goal is to extract meaningful bits of "who" and "why" from the raw data and file them into columns that you'll create as you go. For example:

Response #1: "I guess you could say that I'm *in charge of the sales and marketing* for our small business, even though I wear plenty of other hats. I'm looking for advice on how I can *put together a great sales team to help us expand our business outside the region.*"

In your *who* sheet, you'd create a "Sales and Marketing" column for answers that fit and put the specific wording—"in charge of sales and marketing"—in the first row below that. In your *why* sheet, you'd create a "Team" column for answers that fall into that general category and place the wording—"expand our business outside the region"—below that.

Who:

Sales and Marketing	
in charge of sales and marketing	

Why:

Team	
expand our business outside the region	

Response #2: "Hey, thanks for writing. I'm excited to see how your team and your services could help an aspiring entrepreneur like me learn how to *take my ideas, quit my day job,* and help me *start a new business pursuing my passion.*"

This person is totally different. They haven't yet started a business, and when they do (eventually) start their own business, they'd be the owner.

Aspirational business owners have different needs than someone who leads sales for a growing business, so what you'll do is spin their responses off into new columns in your sheets:

Who:

Sales and Marketing	Owner
in charge of sales and marketing	start a new business

Why:

Team	Start
expand our business outside the region	take my ideas / pursuing passion

Response #3: "I'm the *CMO of our advertising agency*. Right now, we're mostly trying to figure out what we could do to *drum up new client work*."

This person, like our first respondent, also works in marketing. So we'd file their unique feedback as a new row in our "Sales and Marketing" column. Unlike the first two respondents, they want help generating leads.

Who:

Sales and Marketing	Owner
in charge of sales and marketing	start a new business
CMO of our advertising agency	

Why:

Team	Start	Leads
expand our business outside the region	take my ideas / pursuing passion	drum up new client work

RECOGNIZING PATTERNS

It doesn't matter what kind of business you run or what kind of customers you serve: retailer, service provider, even a coworking space or café. We all benefit from asking our customers the right questions and then finding patterns in the answers. Though manual and a bit tedious, this is a fantastic way for you to understand *in their own words* who your customers, both current and future, are and what they need from you. It goes without saying that most of us operate off gut assumptions. These are our customers. This is what they want. But, by spending the time to listen to, analyze, and file these individual responses, you'll gain remarkable insights into the types of people you're actually serving.

What you're looking for are patterns. What are people saying again and again and again? And which ones are outliers that you can safely exclude from the big picture? Throughout this exercise, you're attempting to reduce a pile of information into a handful of core segments, no more than four or five, that you can use to profile your customers. Not everyone will be a fit and that's okay.

Some people have totally different ways of describing the same thing. Use that. Ultimately, the unfiltered feedback you're correlating to specific segments can later be used to better communicate and relate to people. You'll be able to describe how your product helps agency owners "drum up more client work" and talk about how working with you will help ambitious entrepreneurs "quit their day job and pursue their passion."

What I love about seeing this in action with the companies I help is how personal and authentic the messages they send become. Vague assumptions about customers are replaced by a solid grasp of the big picture. A curious entrepreneur can personally follow up with a specific respondent, asking them, for example, to dig deeper into what "pursuing your passion" really means for them, why it's important, and how they can help realize that goal. Customers love the change. It brings a whole added level of meaning to everything your company does.

Done right, I've never seen this process backfire. People are fed up with sterile, robotically emailed Net Promoter Score (NPS) surveys: "On a scale of 1–10, how likely are you to refer this company?" Surveys rarely, if ever, focus on *you*. They are intended only to serve the company doing the surveying. Show people that you sincerely want to understand their needs and they will happily carve out a minute or two to tell you exactly what you want to know.

Through this process, SPI was able to turn this seemingly flat list of emails into a rich, segmented, constantly course-correcting database offering an unprecedented window into their audience. It's the difference between an anthill and an ant farm. With everything finally visible, his team's entire content strategy changed for the better.

USING YOUR NEWFOUND SEGMENTATION SUPERPOWERS

Throughout the remainder of this book, I'll show you how to automatically assign *future* leads and customers into the various discrete segments you've now started to identify. But before you do that, you're going to want to segment your unsegmented or poorly segmented existing list.

There are a number of technical ways to accomplish this, and how you segment your existing list will largely depend on the email marketing software you're using and the experience you want your customers to have. For example, you could do much of this segmentation entirely over email by using special "link triggers" that allow people to self-segment without ever leaving their inbox. They just click the link that represents their answer to a question and your database is updated automatically. Or you could link people to a survey that captures an array of answers at once.

Let's look at how to start the conversation around personalized marketing, and beginning to segment your email list, with your audience:

A few weeks ago, we sent out an email asking you to share with us a bit more about what you're looking for from us. We received so much great feedback. We're now more confident than ever about how we can give you exactly what you're looking for and nothing else.

In order to better personalize your experience with us, we've created a quick, one-minute survey that will ensure we're able to send you the right information, products, and more.

A simple email like this performs well. It shows that you're listening and eager to help. Just tweak it to match your brand's voice (see chapter five) and to ensure it serves as a natural follow-up to the email I asked you to send earlier in this chapter, the one asking customers to describe who they are, what kind of business they run, and what they want from you.

Expect response rates to be higher than the original survey email you sent out. Instead of asking for open-ended feedback, you're giving customers easy-to-answer multiple-choice questions. You can expect around 30 percent of engaged list subscribers to segment themselves, and these happen to be the ones most likely to really read your emails and sales pages.

In the next chapter, you're going to learn how to start segmenting future email list subscribers. For now, give yourself a huge pat on the back. Once you send your initial segmentation email, you'll be well on your way to delivering more relevant and useful messages to your audience. This step alone will put you light-years ahead of your competition, the majority of whom still treat their audience as one homogenous persona. You will finally know who's on your list and what they each really need. Combined with the data you're already storing—purchase history, for example—you're much closer to finding that middle ground between high-touch, one-on-one selling, and low-touch, "say the same thing to everyone" broadcast marketing.

Ultimately, every customer wants to know: How can this help me? With segments, you're going to be able to show them how with unparalleled authenticity and specificity. In the following chapters, I'll show you how to use segments to customize the way you communicate in a number of remarkable ways. The end result will surprise you with its effectiveness and delight your customers with its usefulness and clarity.

Chapter 4

BUILDING YOUR AUDIENCE

No one has ever woken up and thought: I want to get more email.

Why is it, then, that so many companies are so obsessed with getting people on their newsletter? Many use an arsenal of forms—pop-ups, slide-ups, sticky bars, and so on—to attempt to get people to join their email list. And while they know why they want someone to get on their list (they can sell to them), there's nothing inherently valuable, and rarely anything desirable, about a company telling you that they'll . . . send you email.

According to a study done by Sumo (creators of a popular suite of opt-in tools), the average opt-in rate for a website is 2 percent.[6] This means that ninety-eight out of one hundred people, the "drive-bys" who visit your website or view your landing pages, will leave and likely never come back. This is terrible, especially since you're spending money to get those visitors—either through human capital or by paying for ads.

In this chapter, we're going to look at optimizing the first stage of your customer life-cycle funnel: Drive-By to Intrigue. How can you get more people who come across your brand in one way or another to self-elect to leave you with a way of contacting them?

It all starts with the offer.

Traditionally, most people think of an offer as something you're selling, like a product or service. And while this is true, anytime you're asking someone to agree to do something, you're presenting them with an offer. Offers have a cost, they can be risky, and they have a potential reward. The more perceived value an offer has, the more valuable it is. The riskier it is, both financially and with the possible time it'll take to really leverage what you're offering, the harder the sell. If what you're offering someone (or some business) can be perceived to potentially make life better, they'll be more willing to go for your offer.

This calculus—the balance between cost, risk, and reward—is weighed. If the reward outweighs the risk and cost, it'll probably be accepted; if it doesn't, it'll be rejected.

This is why so many "Join our newsletter" opt-in forms go unfilled. What's the reward? The upside? Agreeing to receive future emails really doesn't come with any, so the website visitor needs to decide for themselves. "What's the likelihood that I'll get more useful stuff like the blog post I just read / video I just watched?" If they decide that there's a solid chance you'll send legitimately useful stuff, then they'll opt in. Otherwise, they're gone. And this is why most websites turn away 98 percent of all visitors.

"But our newsletter is free!"

Not so fast. While you're probably not attaching a credit card payment form to your newsletter opt-in forms, you are asking for someone to pay with their time and write-rights to their inbox.

Remember: people are already overwhelmed with email. Why is it a perk to get more of it? It's not. What we need to do is come up with an offer that's so good that more than two out of one hundred are willing to give you write-rights to their inbox. To do this, we need to stop "selling" the newsletter.

CREATING YOUR OFFER

What you need is a highly valuable product that you can sell for time and attention. This is a product that you'll offer on your website, put behind paid ads, promote on podcast episodes, and syndicate on partner websites. And this product will be a series of personalized emails, carefully curated and deliberately structured, that forms an incredible offer that convinces drive-bys to take that next step.

What you'll be offering will be:

- **Contained.** "Here's exactly what you'll get."
- **Transformative.** "After you go through and apply what I have to offer, here's how things will be different for you."
- **Low Impact.** "For the next fourteen days, we'll send you easy-to-follow, personalized lessons that'll help you . . ."
- **Follow-Up.** "If you liked what I covered in this podcast episode on the dos and don'ts of weight loss, you'll love our free, in-depth . . ."
- **Empathetic.** "We know that you've been struggling . . ."

For example, rather than placing a "Get more content like this by joining our newsletter" form at the footer of your blog, you'd instead create an offer that's designed to perfectly tie into what someone needs most right now.

Back when I was running my first software company, Planscope, I invested a bunch of time and money into creating content and SEO. This ultimately led me to get a steady amount of traffic from

Google. These were people who were going to a search engine and typing in things like "how do I get clients?" or "what should I put in a web designer proposal?" I'd often be a top result for those sorts of queries.

The business owner in me wanted these people to sign up for, and ultimately buy, my project management software. After all, producing the content they found wasn't free, and I wanted this content to bring me customers. But when I tried to get people to first check out Planscope and later join the Planscope newsletter, nothing stuck. Opt-in rates were horrendous. And of the people who actually did end up joining the email list, very few of them ever turned into customers.

The problem was with my offer. When someone arrived on my blog and read an article on writing effective web design proposals, they were not researching project management software. They were hunting for information about proposals. In retrospect, it made sense why so few people joined my email list—what I was offering (project management software) had zilch to do with what they obviously needed (help winning a proposal).

I decided to stop trying to get people to sign up for Planscope. Instead, I decided to try to get people to join my newsletter. But the question still stood: What does signing up for "free emails" (whatever that means) from some unknown company (Planscope) have to do with someone's struggle to win this proposal?

It wasn't until I started to think like a drive-by visitor from Google that things started to finally click. Here were people looking for information about freelancing . . . getting clients, pricing their work, writing proposals, and so on. While these people were squarely in my target audience (Planscope was designed to be used primarily by freelancers), most weren't actually looking for software.

I then decided to ditch my failing list-building efforts and create a "5 Days to Better Freelancing" email course. The premise was that in less than a week I'd deliver a series of hard-hitting email lessons that would help the average freelancer get better clients, make more money, and live a happier life freelancing. While this was under the umbrella of Planscope the software company, it had zero to do with the software itself. My goal was to provide the average drive-by on my website with an obvious next step that had broad appeal. Planscope could, and would, come later.

Ultimately, you're going to still offer an opt-in form and ask someone for (at a minimum) their first name and email address. But rather than promoting it as permission to send emails at some point in the future, you'll offer something that's highly valuable and specific to what they're looking for, and with immediate delivery (rather than having them wait until the next time you send a newsletter).

As we'll unpack as we get further through this book, you'll still end up with newsletter subscribers. But rather than leading with a newsletter, you'll instead entice people to self-select to join your audience with something a bit more valuable to them. Strategically, this will serve to properly onboard new people into your brand.

A mistake I often see is that many email marketers throw their "live" emails at everyone, ranging from their most stalwart, long-term customers to subscribers who just found out about them an hour ago. From the perspective of a brand-new subscriber, it's a bit like being thrown headfirst into a rushing torrent of information. Whatever you send today ends up in their inbox, and this probably isn't what they need to hear from you right now.

GROWING YOUR EMAIL LIST

After you have an idea of the offer, or offers, you'll use to build your audience, the next step is to figure out how you'll use these offers to convert those "drive-by" website visitors into new subscribers.

There are a number of ways to technically do this—and we'll get into all of them shortly—but I want to first discuss the three primary means that people end up getting email from organizations like yours.

Landing Pages

These are web pages that serve a single purpose: to get someone to fill out their name, email address, and possibly more.

Structurally, they tend to be pretty bare bones. You'll find a strong, to-the-point headline, a focused sub-headline, and usually some sort of "hero" element—like a video or photo. The copy and content will be punchy, and the focus of the page will be to get someone to fill out the form. These pages usually lack navigation or anything that could distract the visitor from filling out the form and clicking away to another page.

Landing pages are best used when paired with traffic that's optimized to convert. The most obvious example is paid ad campaigns. Marketers are typically spending money, sometimes quite a bit of it, per click. The ad's going to drive someone to some page on their website, and the best place to send someone to is going to be a focused, dialed-in landing page that's designed to get as many people to fill out the form as possible.

How to Create a Great Landing Page

First, you'll want to decide how you technically want to host your landing page. Depending on what your website is built with, it might be as easy as creating a new "Page" in your content management system.

Regardless of your website's content management system (or lack thereof), you can always use a hosted platform like Leadpages or Unbounce. These platforms provide a number of tested templates that you can customize and then easily integrate with your email marketing platform of choice. If you're not technical, or you want something built *quickly* (which isn't a bad idea when you're first testing out a new offer), then I'd recommend using a hosted platform.

The copy on your landing page trumps all other aspects of the page. There are plenty of "bad"-looking web pages that do perfectly well because the copy is so strong. So go with a tested, well-designed template *but* don't skimp on the copy.

The headline of your landing page should reflect what brought someone to it. Landing pages don't exist in a vacuum; no one opens a web browser and randomly stumbles upon these pages. Rather, they are sent to people—from ads, from conference talks, from social media, and more.

Your landing page should reiterate the action that brought someone to the page. If they clicked on an ad targeting stay-at-home moms with a special offer on an energy multivitamin, the headline should repeat, sometimes verbatim, the ad copy that they clicked on. There shouldn't be any disconnect between the intent someone had in clicking on an ad and the content on the page they're brought to. (You'll sometimes see very specific ads that bring people to the home-page for a brand. This should never be done.)

If you're giving a talk at a conference, and you pitch your opt-in offer at the end of your presentation, the landing page you send your audience should be specific for them. For example, if you just gave a killer presentation on emerging financial regulations at the "Midwest-ern Bankers Association Expo," the standout headline on your offer landing page should reference *this* expo, ideally with something obvi-ous like: "Want to learn more about how politicians in Washington are changing the way midwestern bankers like you work? Download my free e-book . . ."

"I freely decided to click on this ad / follow up on this YouTube video's call to action" are strong signals that can play into early pro-filing efforts. Ad platforms like Facebook allow for easy demographic targeting, and broad campaigns should be divided into focused efforts that target key segments and personas.

A great example of this is an online jewelry retailer that I con-sulted with a few years back. Most people who clicked on their ads and visited their website were either looking for an engagement ring or some sort of anniversary present for their partner. While the Face-book ads they were running were doing well at getting people to their website and buying, they knew they could do better. They took their ad campaigns and subdivided them to target three core demographics:

- Single men who are in a relationship
- Single women who are in a relationship
- Married men

People tend to open up to platforms like Facebook and willingly provide data about their relationships, gender, and so on. This allows dynamic marketers like you and me to leverage this data to run very focused ads. We can then use these focused ads to send people to very focused landing pages. This jewelry company sent single men to a landing page that was all about "popping the big question." It featured a large image of a young guy on his knees proposing to his sweetheart. The ads targeting single, but committed, women were focused on a very different thing: finding that picture-perfect engagement ring and nudging your partner to "check it out." Finally, married men would see a distinctly different message. They saw a photo of a very happy, but middle-aged, couple enjoying a bottle of wine together. The headline? "Find the perfect anniversary gift to show the woman you love how much she still means to you."

These three messages, each of which is saying a very different thing, wouldn't work as catch-all messages. The anniversary-focused message put in front of an unmarried young man would fall on deaf ears. But by making assumptions about the *type* of people who arrive at these various landing pages—knowing full well of the targeted ads that have been set up to route different demographics to different pages—you can apply a bit of early segmentation without ever needing to survey or otherwise ask someone online about their relationship status or gender.

Cambridge Analytica[7] was hired by the Trump Campaign for President to do something that was so obvious and so powerful that, once uncovered, resulted in quite the scandal. Cambridge Analytica helped the campaign by running a series of online ads that appealed to the various subsets of conservative voters:

- Low tax
- Pro-life
- Second Amendment
- Anti-regulation
- "Family values"

People would be asked, either through clicks or through explicit surveying, which mattered most to them. And then all subsequent communication from the Trump campaign would largely be dialed in on that *one* issue. Considering how many voters are single-issue voters, it's pretty obvious why this worked so well. "Trump, the anti-abortion hero," is going to fire up ardent pro-lifers in a way that might end up being received indifferently, or even with hostility, by other would-be Trump voters.

When deciding on the landing page you'll be setting up for each of your offers, it probably makes sense to instead think in terms of *pages*. You're probably going to eventually want to have quite a few pages, each sent traffic by a particular set of ads, a particular event you appeared at, a particular podcast episode you were interviewed on, and so on.

Make it clear what happens next. After showing someone that they're at the right place by bridging the action that brought them to your offer page with the headline on the page, you now need to show them what's in it for them to give you whatever information you're asking for.

Your landing page is like a bridge. Its job is to bring someone from where they are *today* to where they need to be *tomorrow*. The headline, and the traffic source (e.g., a specific ad), contribute in a major way to contextualize what *today* is and all the pains, worries, and annoyances that accompany it. Once contextualized, you now need to determine how to best lay out what the path to tomorrow looks like.

This is what the offer you've created does. Your offer is designed to bridge the gap for someone who is afflicted by a specific type of problem and identifies in a particular way. The job of the supporting copy on the landing page—that is, everything around the opt-in form—is to reinforce the need, urgency, and assurance of reaching this tomorrow.

How will opting in to your offer help this person, given what you might know about them (or assume about them)? How specifically will it transform something about their lives? For businesses, how will it help them increase revenue or decrease costs? And for individuals, how will it help them shore up their own hierarchy of needs?

Create trust. Can you show logos of companies who you can claim as clients? How about testimonials or micro case studies of people who have benefited from what you're offering on this landing page?

The people arriving on this landing page probably don't know you. And by asking them to opt in, you're opening up their inbox to even more *stuff*. The more you can do to show that you're reputable, the better. There are few better ways of doing this than showing actual people who have been transformed by what you're offering. This social proof shouldn't be as mundane as, "Wow, these emails were fun to read!"—but should instead encapsulate the before and after: "Every morning I woke up exhausted. But thanks to what I learned about diet and habits in this email course, I'm now waking up refreshed and motivated. Thank you!"

Opt-In Forms

Every lead capture landing page has a form on it. It's where the visitor keys in their name and email address, and clicks a flashy button labeled something like "Subscribe."

List-building forms don't need to exist solely on landing pages, though. They can be added alongside anything on your website, or even layered on top of it. Manifesting as pop-ups, slide-ups, "sticky bars," or embedded forms, marketers have come up with an astonishingly large number of designs and uses for opt-in forms.

Generally speaking, the exact same rules that apply for a landing page exist for regular forms. The key difference is *context*. If you're going to show someone a pop-up that appears when they go to leave your website, you're going to want to think: "This person is about to bail. What do I say to try to convince them otherwise?"

A great opt-in form is going to have a few key elements:

- **A strong, benefit-focused headline *contextualized* to the content.** Is someone leaving the website? Viewing your pricing page? Reading a blog article on time management? How can your opt-in offer "upsell" the visitor to then take that next step? For example, if they're reading an article on time management, "Grab our time management cheatsheet" would be a compelling thing to do next.

- **A sub-headline that includes more details and relevance.** What's in this cheatsheet? What can they expect to be able to do with it? Your headline lured them in, now you need to make it clear why they shouldn't just ignore your form.

- **The form itself.** At a minimum, an email address. The button shouldn't say "Submit," unless you're offering something related to BDSM.

- **An expectation.** What happens after they submit the form? Will you start sending them junk? If they hate what you're sending, will they be able to unsubscribe? Make it clear that you're going to give them something super valuable really quickly, and that you're going to guard this relationship by not abusing their trust.

Join my free course on growing your web design agency?

Thousands of fellow agency owners have completed my 9-lesson email course, *Charge What You're Worth*. No fluff inside – just highly actionable lessons that will help you learn how to better sell your agency to clients.

Your email address...   Send Lesson #1

Most email marketing platforms include opt-in forms that you can use, and many of them are pretty nice and flexible. However, there's a wide variety of plug-ins and stand-alone software that can let you design and build the ultimate opt-in form for your brand, and then integrate it nicely with your email platform of choice.

SEGMENTING NEW SUBSCRIBERS

When someone joins your list, either by opting in via a landing page or because of a form that you've included somewhere on your website, you're going to want to know more than just their email address and first name.

This entire book is predicated on having segmentation information attached to your subscribers—specifically *who* they are and *why* they joined your list. With just an email address and a first name, you cannot make your emails personal. You won't be able to show industry-specific case studies, products that align with their unique needs, and so on. Unfortunately, however, most email marketers are *still* just collecting the basics. Let's find out how to fix that.

What Should You Add to Your Forms?

The most obvious way to get more information about new subscribers is to add more fields to your forms.

These will usually be select fields, where only one option can be selected at a time. With the form shown on the next page, you'll get:

- Email address
- Name
- Favorite food to eat (in this case, their *who*—here's the kind of food examples they'll want to see)
- Cooking struggle (their *why*—what's their biggest impediment to cooking healthy food at home?)

This can then be used to deliver a largely bespoke experience to them over email, making them feel right at home on your email list.

The downside to adding fields to your forms is that it adds more friction to signing up. Opt-in forms are usually designed to convert the maximum number of visitors as possible into subscribers. Punchy, benefit-focused headlines; slick imagery; and a very, *very* simple form are all established best practices for getting more people to join your list. Asking people to think—*What kind of food DO I like? What DO*

Download our free cookbook!

Your email address...

What's your favorite food to cook?

What do you hate about cooking?

Download Now

I hate about cooking?—can surprisingly lead to a high abandonment rate, which can cause your opt-in rate to plummet.

Quizzes

Another segmentation and lead-generation technique is creating quizzes. Chanti Zak, the "Quiz Funnel Queen," has helped a number of companies replace their usual opt-in forms with quiz funnels.[8] She helped TONIC Site Shop develop the "brand cocktail" quiz, which has generated an excess of $50,000 in sales from the quiz alone. She also helped Jenna Kutcher add more than one hundred thousand new subscribers with a quiz.

From the perspective of the person taking the quiz, the benefit is that by giving up a few bits of information, you'll be routed to exactly what you need. You'll often find quizzes used on e-commerce stores for

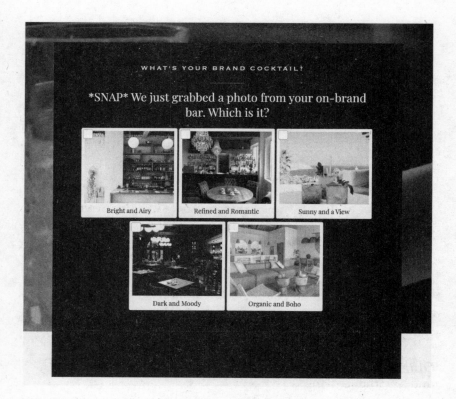

helping people find their perfect outfit or whatever else. It allows the brand to recommend a next step given some key information, rather than leaving it up to the visitor to browse through a catalog of products.

But for the team creating the quiz, quizzes are a treasure trove of segmentation data. Many quizzes end with an opt-in form, asking the visitor to enter their name and email address to get their result. When set up correctly, a new subscriber will be added with a name and email address, and this new subscriber will also have *all* the associated segmentation data (i.e., answers to questions) enriching their new record.

And unlike forms, which are generally static, a quiz can have conditional follow-up questions. If you answer that "spicy" is your favorite type of food, the next question could ask you to select your favorite spicy food. You can't easily and elegantly do this on a normal opt-in form.

Post-Opt-In Surveys

While I love quizzes, they're not always the right tool for the job. Sometimes people just want to join the newsletter or download your free report without jumping through the hoops of needing to answer a bunch of questions.

An alternative approach, which largely has the same end result, is to replace your usual opt-in confirmation page with a survey. This means that when someone joins your email list, rather than sending them to a page that says something like, "Thanks! Go check your email," you send them to a survey that aims to find out who they are and why they're here.

At RightMessage, we're doing exactly this. You join our free email course and you're shown a simple questionnaire that starts with a rather inoffensive question: "If we could help you do just ONE thing, what would that be?"

Because we don't want to stand in the way of them receiving the first lesson of the course they've enrolled for, we show a five-minute countdown timer that lines up with when our email system will send the first email. By answering these questions before the course kicks off, the content they get from us will be much more personally relevant to them. As we put it, "We want to make sure we're sending you exactly what you need (and nothing more!)."

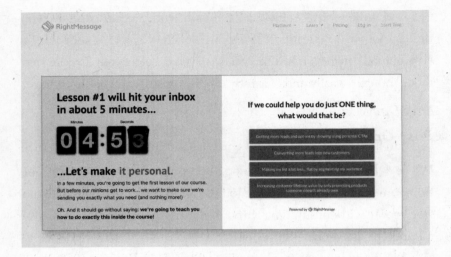

More than 80 percent of all new subscribers to the RightMessage email list complete this survey. For these subscribers, we know:

— What their goal is in joining our list
— What kind of business they run
— What email platform (if any) they use
— If they don't use an email platform, what's holding them back?
— Otherwise, are they happy with their daily list growth? How are they getting new subscribers? And how effective are their email marketing efforts?

This segmentation data ends up being used to deliver a highly personal email course that people love. While what we teach is largely consistent for everyone, people who use ConvertKit and run a coaching business will see different examples, different case studies, and different language than someone else who runs an online store and uses Klaviyo. If we didn't ask these questions after someone joined our course, we'd need to give the exact same content to everyone, which would alienate our readers ("if THIS affects you . . . or THAT affects you . . . or maybe THIS . . .").

Link Surveys

You can also segment someone entirely from within your email marketing software, and without the expense of paying for quiz or survey software or adding a lot of friction, by adding additional fields to opt-in forms.

This is done by adding what are called "link triggers." These are special links that virtually all email platforms support that, when clicked, can further segment a subscriber. When someone clicks a link trigger in an email you sent them, any associated actions—like tagging the subscriber as someone who likes the color yellow—are performed on the subscriber's record, and then they're sent along to the web page that the link points to.

Link surveys are constructed just like normal email content. Usually, you'll have a bolded question like, "Which of the following best describes . . ." And then you'd show a list of bullet points, with each bullet point including a link trigger that performs segmentation and then brings the subscriber to some sort of generic "thanks for your feedback" page on your website.

Link surveys have two big drawbacks.

First off, you can only add one question per email. It would be awkward to ask five different questions in a single email, and to expect someone to click their answer for the first question, be taken to the feedback page in their web browser, head back to your email and click the answer to the second question, and so on and so forth.

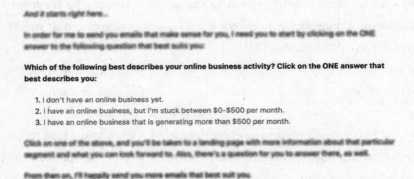

And, finally, link surveys tend to get really low engagement rates. When surveying email marketing peers of mine who regularly use link surveys, the average click rate is something like 30 percent—which means that a minority of your subscribers end up being segmented. And while there's room for link surveys to be used to collect passive data over time and unobtrusively, I wouldn't really recommend it for something as important as the *who* and *why* segmentation questions that will end up driving the entire experience a new subscriber has with your brand.

YOUR NEWFOUND SUPERPOWER

You'll recall that I originally thought that, since the job of a software company is to sell software, I should be focused on marketing free trials to Planscope. Demographically aligned people (that is, freelancers) would google around for information on freelancing, find some article of mine I published on the Planscope blog, and (assuming they finished the article) would be shown an ad for a free trial.

This obviously didn't work all that well. Those looking for information weren't being pitched on something relevant to them. It wasn't until I started to promote the call to action to join a free crash course on freelancing that I started to see both higher engagement and higher quality. What was being offered was so much more aligned with what the actual people consuming my content were looking for.

However, I still made one crucial mistake: I captured a first name and an email address, but that was it. Beyond greeting people by their first names in emails, everyone was treated identically. I didn't do any sort of segmentation. But that was perfectly normal. No one did then. Fast-forward a decade, and sadly not much has changed. Most email opt-ins show subscribers a boring confirmation message. Some might present some sort of initial pitch, usually a rather inexpensive offer with a heavy time-sensitive discount attached (what internet marketers call a "trip wire"), designed to turn that new subscriber into a new customer as soon as possible. But actually learning about the individual wants and needs of your new subscribers . . . ?

By following what I covered in this chapter, you'll go beyond average and show your audience that you're committed to listening. Your fans and customers want to know they're being heard. Present your questions clearly, and they'll know that you're surveying them so that you can better help them. What you capture becomes your newfound superpower. It enables you to tweak and tailor both your messaging and the products you offer to be more personally relevant to the individual on the receiving end.

Only after internalizing that this *is* a new relationship will this all make sense—that is, someone raises their hand and says, "Yes, I want to hear more from this brand! But I also want to have my say."

Relationships are built on mutual understanding. You need to make an effort to understand your audience, discovering a bit about why they joined your email list and what their current situation is. If you don't do this, you have no other recourse but to treat everyone on your list identically. That would work. You *will* get sales (after all, this is the default behavior for just about every brand that does email marketing). But you won't get as many sales as you could. Irrelevant communication leads to people tuning out and thinking they're at the wrong place.

The rest of this book is now going to be focused on wielding this new superpower. How do you use this information about each individual subscriber to deliver better, more relevant content? Most importantly, how do you use this knowledge to win more customers and *consistently* increase your sales?

Chapter 5

ROLL OUT THE WELCOME MAT

American megachurches fascinate me.

While I'm not particularly religious, I was brought up in a church-going household. Every Sunday, we piled into the family Suburban and drove over to Calvary Chapel, which had recently taken over a massive plot of land and relabeled it as a "campus." Soon, they'd set up a coffee shop, restaurant, and boasted a congregation of more than 20,000 weekly attendees and a staff of more than 350.

In my hometown of Fort Lauderdale, the meteoric growth of the church turned heads. My schooling was at more traditional Methodist and Presbyterian private schools, and even as a kid I remember hearing disgruntled, offhand remarks from the staff about "Calvary poaching more of our parishioners . . ."

How did Calvary Chapel, along with all the other megachurches, grow so quickly? Weekly church attendance had been slowly declining in the United States for decades. What were they doing that the more traditional, mainline churches largely weren't? Putting aside theological differences, what was their "secret sauce"?

Now, I'm the most lay of laypeople. I have no immediate knowledge of how churches grow. I've never been hired by a church. But I have spent a lot of time in churches. When I finally got my driver's license, my parents still required me to go to church weekly, but the church I chose was totally up to me. Having sat through two-hour-long church services for the last decade, sixteen-year-old me discovered that the local Roman Catholic parish down the street had fifty-minute church services. Perfect!

This church, however, was objectively dying. I was the only parishioner still sporting their natural hair color. New people would occasionally show up, but rarely did I ever see them come back. With each Sunday's bulletin listing out another funeral or three, I couldn't see how the parish would survive another decade.

Yet the evangelical megachurch down the road, Calvary Chapel Fort Lauderdale, kept growing, and growing, and growing.

I have a theory. It has to do with how new people are treated.

At weekly Mass, the priest at the Roman Catholic parish I'd chosen would celebrate the Mass per the usual rubrics. Right before the homily, he'd rattle through the upcoming spaghetti dinner night, a bingo event, and whatever else. He'd quickly highlight that after the Mass there'd be donuts and coffee and that if you were new, you should feel free to partake.

Calvary's approach was totally different. If you were new, you were hunted down. Being thrown headfirst into a massive audience of people who know the church, know all the pastor's inside jokes, and know the *process* is hugely intimidating. The "growth" staff, or whatever title they had for themselves, knew this. New visitors would be asked to raise their hands at some point during the service. Other attendees would enthusiastically clasp their hands and welcome the newcomers to Calvary. Dedicated staff would also try to make note of where the newcomers were sitting. After the service, they would encourage new visitors to join one of the local bible study groups.

It really was pretty genius. New visitors were placed into existing cohorts of people who mostly lived in the same neighborhood. This would immediately give new visitors a new group of friends who, on subsequent Sundays, could seek each other out and talk about last night's football game (or whatever else churchgoers small talk about). Someone at the church would also be assigned the task of intentionally acclimating the new parishioner to the beliefs of the church, updating them on the things happening each week, and sharing other pertinent information.

Almost immediately, a new visitor felt a sense of belonging. They'd joined a small, intimate group of other churchgoers who just happened to live in their neighborhood. Getting familiar with the church wasn't left to chance and time: a dedicated stakeholder made it their mission to pass along the "Calvary way" as quickly as possible. In a culture that desperately lacks community and belonging, should any of us be surprised that Calvary Chapel is siphoning off so many churchgoers in South Florida?

This is such an important lesson in marketing, and it's one that directly applies to email marketing.

When someone decides to join your email list, they're giving you two things:

1. **Permission:** They're giving you their contact information and allowing you to talk, learn, and sell to them.
2. **Attention:** Unless they opted in under dubious circumstances, the fact is they're somewhat intrigued at this point. You lured them in with a compelling free gift—your opt-in offer—and now they want to hear more about how you're able to help them.

Unfortunately, *so* many brands drop the ball here. They add someone to their email list . . . and go mostly silent, or at least haphazard and random with their communication. Or they go über-promotional and take the attitude of "s#%! or get off the pot" when it comes to being a subscriber to their email list.

In this chapter we're going to explore how to properly onboard and acclimate new people to your brand.

This means we're going to think through and execute on how to show someone they're at the right place and joined the right email list, that you understand what it is they need from you, and that you have a road map for connecting the dots.

This road map is best thought of as a plan for how you'll deliver more than they ask for. Practically speaking, this means how you'll send someone illuminating and important information that legitimately helps them. The intended outcome is that the resulting "value equation" is unbalanced: you've given them way more than they've given you. The amount of help and eye-openers you've delivered them far outweighs the attention they've paid you. Those five-hundred-word emails that took just minutes to read every few days? The takeaway from those emails is massive, which makes the time spent opening your emails and reading through them a no-brainer.

Here's why this imbalance is so important: you want to make it clear that when someone invests in your brand, the payoff far exceeds the cost. While the only real cost so far has been their time and your intrusion into their inbox, you want this perceived imbalance to persist throughout the entire relationship with this person. Currently they might just be a free subscriber who's really loving your emails, but eventually you want them to become a paying customer. And you want to make it obvious (sometimes with a bit of prodding, which we'll talk about later) that your brand's a multiplier: give you time or money, and what you'll give them ends up being a lot more valuable.

This is going to be the imbalance that we attempt to strike throughout the onboarding process. While, yes, we ultimately want to have license to pitch someone on all of our products and services available, we want to first establish trust. This is done by sending relevant and useful content and sending it regularly. There are a number of different ways to do just this, which we'll look at now.

A QUICK NOTE ON EMAIL AUTOMATION

I want this book to be timeless. The principles covered are deeply rooted in the human psyche and haven't changed in millennia. One danger in reading a business book like this that's been published for a while is coming across stale material—for example, if I read a book on online marketing today (2023) and there was an entire chapter dedicated to using MySpace, I'd . . . well, I'd question the applicability of the book.

While I want this book to be genuinely useful no matter *when* you read it, I do need to talk briefly about some of the technicalities of email marketing software. Fortunately, I don't see much of what I'm about to say changing anytime soon.

When you're communicating with your audience, there are really two main mechanisms for doing this: broadcast and via life-cycle automation.

Broadcast messaging is what we used to call "email blasts." It's a one-off email, sent either to your entire list or a sub-segment of your list, that is written and sent either immediately or sometime in the future. This is the online marketing equivalent of drafting a new email in your inbox and BCC'ing a bunch of people.

Life-cycle automation is when messages are dispatched relative to something occurring, what we'll call a *trigger*. Triggers include joining your email list for the first time, abandoning a shopping cart, becoming a customer, or having a birthday. These life-cycle automations are started with a trigger, and then usually are made up of a series of delays and emails. For example: Someone buys from you for the first time and they *immediately* get a "Thanks for being a customer!" email alongside their automated receipt email. Then, a day later, they get a "Could you rate your shopping experience?" email request. And two days after that, they get another email with an upsell. These automated emails are sent relative to a triggering action, and their sending is fully handled by a machine. Some marketer strung together the automation along with the emails contained within, published it, and now it's running on its own.

What we're going to cover in this chapter on rolling out the welcome mat is going to be backed by automation. Each example

I'm about to show you has a trigger, and that's almost always "someone joined your email list."

But I regrettably can't show you *how* to actually use your email platform of choice to set up these automations. That's going to be the job of the help center for your software, along with any other technical training materials they provide. Each platform has some way of setting up automated campaigns, but the language used to describe what's going on and the process used to set it all up is going to change. And continue to change—long after this book has been released.

Don't worry too much about if you're not a pro email marketer or have no desire to become one. I've designed this book to be able to be applied in a big-picture sort of way that incorporates both *business* (for you) and *technical* (for whoever does the work, which could be you!) strategy. Should you decide to have others set up and manage your email marketing and write your email copy, you'll be able to take the framework I teach in this book, apply it to your unique business and goals, and then hand it off to whoever.

THE IMMERSION SEQUENCE

We'll start with a basic sequence that fulfills all the requirements I outlined at the beginning of this chapter.

This is primarily designed for opt-in offers that don't specifically provide anything, like joining your newsletter. Rather than throwing someone headfirst into your content calendar, where they begin receiving whatever promotions or other content you're sending out to your entire list, you'll first spend some time welcoming them to your brand.

It's important to recognize that when someone first opts in to your email list, they're highly engaged. After all, they just said, "Yes, you may send me emails," and while they might not *fully* trust you yet, this is the time to do exactly that—send them emails. The automated Immersion Sequence emails you send out should be spaced a day apart, with the first one being sent immediately after they join your email list.

Here's a general outline of what you should be sending:

- Immediately: *You're at the Right Place*
- +1 day: *Here's What You'll Become*
- +1 day: *Here's Someone Like You*
- +1 day: *Here's What's Next*

Now let's look at each email in depth.

You're at the Right Place

In this first email, you want to use your newfound segmentation superpowers and make it crystal clear that someone didn't end up making a mistake by giving you their email address.

Your number-one email marketing enemy is churn. These are the people who decide to unsubscribe from your emails and never hear from you again. But an equally important enemy is apathy. You don't want people getting your emails and just ignoring them, or opening, skimming, and immediately archiving. What you want is an engaged audience. People who consume what you send, buy when you ask them to buy, and refer others because they think you're the bee's knees.

To counter both churn and apathy, you're going to need to use the very first email you send someone to set the benchmark of quality. It needs to be highly personal and relevant. It needs to show someone they're at the right place.

Here's how I recommend you do this.

As we discussed in the last chapter, when someone first joins your email list you want to use this as an opportunity to find out a bit more about them. Ideally you want to uncover *who* they are (identity) and *why* they're here (need). Because you're collecting this when someone joins your email list, you'll either have this data—assuming you're asking it as part of your opt-in form—or you'll have coverage for the majority of new subscribers if you collect this segmentation data on your opt-in form's confirmation page.

You want your very first email to be opened. And the best way to do this is to make sure that the subject line of this email reflects their primary need. Let's say you run a lawn care company and your opt-in uncovers that a person is struggling with weeds (as opposed to dead grass or pests). The very first email you send should scream, "We're going to eliminate your weed problem." That's *all* you want to focus on right now.

Your first email's subject line should be something like: "Lawn overrun with weeds? We're here to help. Here's how . . ."

This subject, compared to two inferior alternatives—"We can help with your lawn problems" and "We can help with your weed, dead grass, and pest problems"—specifically references the exact problem they shared with you. This is exactly what would happen in reality, isn't it? If you asked a salesperson at a lawn care company to get in touch because your grass was mostly made up of weeds, they'd probably kick off the conversation with something like: "So, your lawn is covered with weeds, huh?"

My friend Joanna Wiebe of Copyhackers, who is probably the best copywriter I've ever met, likes to say that the job of every line of copy is to get someone to keep reading. The more likely someone is to read your entire email, the better the chance that they get something useful out of it. More usefulness means higher engagement. And people with high engagement are unlikely to churn out by unsubscribing from your email list.

So, every line of copy in this first email, *especially* the copy at the top of the email, is vitally important. I want to share with you an example of a *You're at the Right Place* email that I created a few years ago. This email changes depending on a few different factors:

— Is this person a full-time freelancer, or are they doing it on the side still?
— What kind of work do they primarily do? Are they a web designer, a programmer, a writer, a marketer, or something else?
— Why does this person want to work for themselves as a freelancer? Is it because they want financial security, more time to spend with their family, more freedom, or because they want to make a difference?
— If they're not full-time yet, what's holding them back?
— And if they are full-time, do they work solo or as part of a team (i.e., they're an agency)?

First off, let me be the first to welcome you to Double Your Freelancing!

We're a community of over 50,000—many of whom are <u>freelance web designers</u> like you.

<u>Jane</u>, this isn't just some standard "autoresponder" email.

Over the next few weeks, I'm going to be sending you fully personalized advice specific to YOU and your situation.

- I'll help you figure out what needs to happen <u>to work full-time for yourself</u> so you can <u>reclaim more of your time.</u>
- For many new freelancers, <u>figuring out where to start is tough.</u> What if you don't get clients? What if you're not good enough? And how much should you charge (and what if people say you're charging too much)? I've coached thousands of freelancers and have a pretty bulletproof framework I'll be laying out over the next few weeks that will help you take your skillset, apply it to client business problems, and leverage smart sales and marketing strategies to keep yourself busy.
- You're a <u>web designer</u>, so I'll make sure the advice I give you applies to the kind of work you do.

In the above email, I'm setting the stage for how someone is going to go through a transformation by being a part of my audience. In this case, it's Jane, a web designer who hasn't yet gone full-time on her own business, isn't sure exactly how to start, and ultimately wants to work for herself so she can spend more time with her family.

The underlines are emphasis that I've included for this book but highlight how we decided to change key bits of the messaging to fit the subscriber. Had this new subscriber been an agency owner who's been doing this for a while and created custom apps for their clients, this messaging would have completely fallen on deaf ears.

This is why so many brands end up dumbing down their messaging, because they need to figure out how to speak equally to Jane the novice freelancer who's a bit unsure of herself, while not losing Kim the owner of a thriving software agency. So those brands who don't have the means to personalize their content end up using phrases like ". . . for freelancers and agencies . . ." and ". . . whether you're just starting a business or already own one . . ." and other examples of finding common-denominator language that doesn't exclude—yet doesn't really speak directly to anyone.

You want this email to show *empathy*—we know who you are, and we know what you're struggling with and how it weighs upon you.

You want it to also show *authority*—we've worked with people exactly like you before.

You want it to show that you're *listening*—you've told us what you need from us, and we want to give you exactly what *you* personally need from us.

And, finally, you want to show them *what's next*—here's what you can expect next from us. (You want your newest subscribers to eagerly await tomorrow's email.)

> Tomorrow I'm going to share with you something that'll help you finally go full-time on your business—it's a 5-step framework that thousands of <u>designers</u> have used.
> Keep an eye out for that email, <u>Jane</u>!

Here's What You'll Become

Now that you've successfully set the stage by sending a highly personalized welcome email, you want to give someone an idea of what's to come *for them.*

The first email you sent contextualized the "today." Here's **where you are** (*not yet working full-time for yourself*). Here's what's **holding you back** (*you're battling internally with doubts on how you'll quit your job and announce to the world that you are your own boss*). And here's why you so **desperately want to cross the chasm** (*you feel like you're spending all your time at the office, and not nearly enough time doing the things that matter*).

Today's email needs to show the World of Tomorrow and set your brand as the hero that'll get them from A to B. You've undoubtedly seen loads of films that take the protagonist, pair them with a wise mentor, and a few montages later a hero emerges? These films all follow the Hero's Journey, first clearly articulated by the late Joseph Campbell. You want to position your brand as that archetypal mentor who's going to bring a person from where they are today to where they need to be tomorrow, taking them from zero to hero.

Let's talk about you.

You shared with me that you're <u>wanting to go full-time</u> on your <u>design freelancing</u> business.

Working for yourself is a process that I went through about ten years ago, and it was not easy. At all.

But it's *so worth it*. Here are a few ways my life has changed since then:

- As a young dad, I'm able to attend pretty much all of my children's events—I'm oftentimes the only dad chaperoning their field trips!
- I'm able to help my wife with the day-to-day house responsibilities.
- I can take time off to go on vacation with my family whenever I want and without needing to ask any-one's permission.
- I've been able to make significantly more money, which gives our family a lot more financial stability.

Now I want to shift gears and talk about a 5-step system that will help you take the plunge from full-time employee to rockin' your own <u>design</u> business . . .

By giving someone a vision of tomorrow, you can start laying out the foundation for the *problem*. This is an important concept that needs to be something you obsess over if you want to be able to successfully sell your products or services over email. You need to make it clear throughout all of your communication, and especially when you go to sell, that there are two outcomes:

- **To continue what they're doing now and stay in the World of Today.** For Jane, the part-time designer, this means to continue to mess around with night and weekend projects that give her even less time with her family.
- **To move to the World of Tomorrow.** Complete owner-ship over Jane's time. More quality time spent with family and friends. The security that comes with knowing that she's her own boss.

The *problem* is what happens if they continue to remain in the World of Today. The solution is to move to the World of Tomorrow. The offer is the thing that connects the two—today and tomorrow—and serves as the bridge that safely moves people from here to there. (We'll be going much deeper into all of this once we start getting into how to sell via email.)

The *Here's What You'll Become* email does something that might seem a bit common sense: to show what happens when today's problems are eliminated. But by being explicit with what effect the removal of those problems has, you show that you understand what's at stake. And you're also able to lead by authority and begin setting your brand up as the ferry pilot who's going to help this new subscriber safely navigate between the World of Today and the World of Tomorrow.

You're going to want to close this email by leveraging your new-found segmentation abilities by letting them know that tomorrow you'll be sending a case study or example story of someone just like them who's done this before.

Here's Someone Like You

I haven't always been an advocate of segmentation and personalization. In fact, there was a time when I sent the same emails and showed the same sales pages to everyone.

And then Maggie came into my life.

It was early in my career as a digital course creator, and my flagship course helped freelancers learn how to price their services. While the course was marketed as a course on pricing, it really was about how to figure out what root problem, or problems, caused a would-be client to reach out to you, and to then use that to determine the potential value of their project. Once you know what a project is worth to a client, you could then anchor your costs through a really effective proposal to position the work you were doing as an investment, rather than an expense.

Anyway, all of this was captured on the sales page, but there was one giant issue that I was oblivious to: all of the testimonials and examples were from people like me. My background is in software development and design. Many, many years ago, I used to build websites and web applications for clients. Most of the people who bought my course early on were people like me—web developers and designers.

But Maggie was a copywriter. She'd heard about my course from a friend who really got a lot out of it, and she decided to check it out. The problem was that she didn't see herself at *all* on the sales page. There was plenty of talk about "raising your rates," and lots of smiling testimonials from people with *developer* or *designer* in their job titles, but Maggie felt like she was in an alien world.

So she decided to send me an email: *"Hey Brennan, I've heard some great things about your course about pricing. I looked over the sales page, but it looks like it's geared toward web developers and web designers. I'm a copywriter . . . can this help me?"*

This email hit me like a sack of bricks. Why? Because the course was totally agnostic with regard to what kind of work a freelancer did! It was focused on how to sell. Whether you sold words, code, design, or whatever else, the same principles equally applied. How many other people had Maggie's doubts, but didn't bother emailing me?

People, when faced with a tough decision, are always inclined to bail. If I'm looking at a product, I'm mentally weighing the impact of the actual cost of the thing, the time I'll need to spend figuring it out, and the potential cost of needing to backtrack: What if this doesn't work and I need to cut my losses and find something else? When faced with this sort of decision, we often try to justify reasons for something not being a sure enough bet. *Can I see myself benefiting from this?* If there's too much uncertainty, the sale is lost.

People like Maggie didn't see themselves in my course. They didn't see other copywriters who had benefited from it. They didn't see the sort of language copywriters used ("fee")—rather, they saw words like "rate" and other bits that didn't reflect the reality of the kind of work they did. And for many copywriters (and marketers, and photographers, and anyone else who didn't define themselves as a developer or designer), it was just too risky. They'd close the tab, walk away, and I'd never hear from them. I'd just see them factored into the overall conversion rate of how many people saw the sales page relative to how many ended up buying.

"But, surely, the fix is to just add copywriter-ish language to your sales material, right?"

My initial thought was exactly this. I need to go broader. I need to eliminate the usage of the word "rate" to represent what someone charges their clients, and instead default to the safety of "price." I need to diversify my testimonials, so they're not just represented by the early customers of the course (who were like me), but were instead composed of a wide variety of freelancers.

But then I remembered a sales discussion I had when working in my previous company. Planscope was web-based project management software. Its target audience was anyone who managed projects for external stakeholders—i.e., clients—and wanted a collaborative platform to show stakeholders what was being worked on, what they were getting charged, and to discuss the details of the project. This meant that the customers were almost exclusively companies that did digital work for clients, and they were either small and solo (freelancers) or part of a team (agencies).

"Anything that could help freelancers couldn't work for *us*." The would-be customer I was talking to, who ran a small design agency, was sitting in on a product demo. I showed them how they'd be able to use our reporting to uncover insights into how well their projects were staying on track, and how consistent they were at budgeting correctly. They were also shown how they'd be able to invite their entire team and see in real time who was working on what. And I wrapped up the pitch with a demonstration of what Planscope would look like for their clients, and how easy it would be for them to use.

". . . anything that could help freelancers couldn't work for *us*."

When he said this at the end of my demo, I was frankly really surprised. The product did everything he needed it to do. What was wrong? The problem, it seemed, was that on the marketing website for Planscope there were testimonials from both freelancers *and* agencies. The product descriptions always used the blanket phrase "freelancers and designers." I really struggled to see what the problem was.

The issue, really, was that he had spent a lot of time building his company to be bigger than himself. He had a team and an office and wanted a hard line in the sand drawn between the initial version of the company (him, the freelancer) and the latest iteration (a growing team with an international portfolio of clients). As someone who used to run a large agency, I totally understood where he was coming from. But I couldn't get my head around how he couldn't see that the product itself works identically for both freelancers and agencies. Sure, the freelancers wouldn't need to invite any team members or look at the same reports, but both freelancers and agencies had to juggle projects, deal with budget overruns, and discuss stuff with their clients—right?

Our positioning was too broad for this agency. They wanted "project management for agencies" and would have probably preferred "project management for design agencies," but we were "project management for freelancers and agencies." And even though on paper we were a perfect match for him, I ended up losing the sale because we weren't exclusively catering to companies like his.

This is ultimately why niched products and services do so well. In a perfect world, you'd buy the product designed just for you. You wouldn't be reading this somewhat broad book on selling with email; you'd instead be reading a book that helps *your industry* along with, ideally, *your job role* at selling more with email. The more niche the product or service, the less risky it is. People see themselves in the offer. They're being spoken to, and there's very little "noise" (that is, examples, language, testimonials, FAQs, or whatever else that doesn't directly apply to them). We all want the perfect product, but it generally doesn't make sense for a software company to niche down so far as to build "project management software for design agencies."

In this pivotal third email, the *Here's Someone Like You* email, you need to drop a story that's highly relevant to the individual reading your emails.

If you've uncovered who they are and why they joined your list, you want to follow up on yesterday's World of Tomorrow email by telling the story of someone who's actually made it successfully to tomorrow. This also makes your email list less about just you and them. They can now see someone else, who looks a lot like them and who has successfully made it from here to there, and they can take comfort in knowing that they *can* do this. That it *is* something attainable.

We all battle with some form of imposter syndrome, and if you're leaving it up to your audience to read between the lines and piece together how what you offer relates to them and can help them, you're going to lose a lot of people. Conversely, if you can make it clear that you're listening to them and their unique needs, that you have a plan for serving them, and that you've worked with people just like them, then you're going to end up with a new subscriber who's absolutely convinced that you "get" them.

And if you get them (and they know it), then the likelihood that they end up thinking that buying from your brand is ultimately worth their while goes up substantially.

Here's What's Next

On the fourth day, you're now going to give people a bit more context into the business your brand sells and other resources that will get them invested in the journey.

I like to use this as an opportunity to do three things:

1. **Soft promote various products or services.** Bonus points for highlighting a specific offer that relates to them and their current *why*.
2. **Deliver links to non-textual resources and other goodies.**
3. **Set expectations.**

Let's look at what these mean in a bit more depth.

Soft Promote Various Products or Services

Don't refrain from promoting what you have for sale, especially when you're able to directly align it to the *why* that brought them to you.

As we'll explore more in later chapters, pitching someone on your products or services shouldn't ever feel like something aggressive. When contextualized by the World of Today and the World of Tomorrow, your products or services need to just be framed as a *better* way of getting from today to tomorrow.

My recommendation here is to bullet list out a few recommended products that make sense for someone early on in their relationship with you.

Deliver Links to Non-textual Resources and Other Goodies

Whether you're a solo operator or representing a large brand, over the last few days your latest subscriber has gotten to know a bit about your personality, your values, and the authority you have in helping them solve their *why*.

Here's your opportunity to get them out of their inbox and over to other opportunities to get even more from you. My recommendations:

- Your YouTube channel, and ideally a "if you only have time to watch one thing from our channel, watch this" video.
- Your podcast (same thing as above: reference a specific episode), or a few appearances you've made on other podcasts.
- Your social media feeds.
- Video reviews from third parties about your brand.
- A link to your book's Goodreads profile.
- A link where people can find unbiased reviews for your business.
- Digital versions of newspaper or magazine articles that feature you.

Not only can this be a great way of putting a face or a voice on your brand (through videos or podcast episodes), but it's also a really effective way of simply stating: *We're established. We're out there.* Email's great (obviously!), but it's one medium. By getting your subscribers to go beyond email and to hear you, physically see you, hear what unbiased past customers have independently said about you, and more, you end up adding a lot more color and context.

Set Expectations

Over the last four days, you've delivered a salvo of highly relevant emails that dialed in on the specific pain point that brought someone to your email list, gave them an idea of how you could make their business or their life better, delivered a specific example of someone who successfully made the transition, and have now added a bit of color to your brand by referencing videos, interviews, and other resources that feature you.

But what happens next?

This is really up to you, and in later chapters we'll talk more about ongoing nurturing. But, for the most part, you want to let your new subscriber know that more is coming.

As you develop additional assets, like email courses or downloadable lead magnets, you could optionally offer these to check out, but for most of us the next step is to now enroll someone onto your newsletter properly and send out information, sales pitches, and more as you develop it.

Regardless of what you do—and like with your entire email system, it's going to change—you want to give your subscribers an idea of what's to come. Do you send a new newsletter every Thursday morning? Or maybe you just announce new events and products?

Whatever it is you plan on doing, give your new subscribers the courtesy of knowing when they'll be hearing from you next. (After all, you've been emailing them daily for the last four days!)

THE LEAD MAGNET ACCOUNTABILITY SEQUENCE

The above Immersion Sequence is a great catch-all for general new additions to your email list. And the principles covered are universal and should be made a part of whatever sort of email list onboarding efforts you make.

But rarely is "join our email list" a compelling, and conversion-optimized, offer. Why? Because no one's ever woken up and thought, "I wish I received more email every day!" People's inboxes are generally overflowing, and the struggle with Inbox Zero is a real concern for most professional and personal inboxes alike. This is why most generic newsletter email opt-ins tend to get a 1.95 percent opt-in rate,[9] while focused opt-ins often see upwards of 5 percent.[10]

A common strategy for companies is to create lead magnets, which are typically downloadable files that are given up in exchange for an email address. Unlike joining an email list, which generally doesn't offer anything of immediate value ("we'll email you . . . sometime . . ."), a lead magnet's value proposition is straightforward: give us your contact information and we'll give you this valuable file.

Lead magnets come in all forms, but here are a few of the most common:

- Free reports
- White papers
- E-books

- Checklists
- Infographics
- Cheat sheets
- Automated, "evergreen" on-demand webinars
- Email courses

While lead magnets obviously work well—the typical conversion rate compared to a baseline email newsletter opt-in is significantly higher—they tend to be sold as a transactional exchange, rather than the start of a long-term relationship. Additionally, many of them end up collecting "digital dust" in people's downloads folder. Sure, that free e-book sounded really interesting and worth opting in for, but the likelihood that it'll actually be read? It's pretty low.

Fortunately, there's an effective way to deliver on all the transformative principles I covered in the last example when delivering a lead magnet. Do this right, and you'll not only end up with more engaged new subscribers, but you'll also get more people to actually *consume* and use the lead magnet they opted in for. And if you recall what I said earlier about the importance of creating offers that outweigh their cost—for example, the takeaways from your free e-book far outweigh the time someone spent reading your e-book—then you absolutely want more consumption. If people tune out your lead magnet, they're probably going to tune out whatever else you have to send them.

The way to do this is to deliver a post-opt-in Accountability Sequence that's designed to walk someone through the thing you sent them. If you deliver a free book, this should be a "virtual book club" of sorts that leads someone through the book, chapter-by-chapter, through a series of emails. These emails should not only reinforce what you teach in the book, but also serve as an opportunity to link back to the book's file at every opportunity. And as with every great book club, it should get people thinking. Attached to each email should either be an easy-to-complete worksheet or a few big-picture questions that you want your readers to consider.

These emails, while ideally being designed to get someone to actively consume and act on the educational material you send, should also introduce your brand, provide social proof and case studies of other people who have gone through a transformation as a result of their relationship with your brand, and also set the right expectations about what's coming next. What you *don't* want to do is just deliver a resource, like a white paper, and then go radio silent for a bit, and a few days later suddenly start bombarding your new subscribers with promotional emails or your live newsletter.

Here are a few ideas of Accountability Sequences that you could use for different types of lead magnets.

- **Free reports:** A few emails that walk someone through each section of the report. These emails should link to resources you used when creating the report, like academic research or other third-party, unbiased source material. You should also provide additional context that wasn't included in the report (especially if it's video or audio material). This will allow you to position the Accountability Sequence as a *premium* add-on to the report someone requested, rather than just a series of drip emails.

- **White papers:** If you're sending someone a white paper that's, say, a guide to purchasing CRM software and *you* sell CRM software, you're going to want to use your Accountability Sequence to link to as much material that's outside the umbrella of your brand as possible. These might be links to comparative digests on review websites like G2 or Trustpilot, along with links to your own product's listing. And as you move through and reinforce the steps a purchaser should take in considering new CRM software, make it clear that these emails *can* be replied to—and that a friendly account executive from your company is ready and waiting should any questions pop up.

- **E-books:** This was covered above, but e-books are naturally broken up into logical chapters, which allows you to easily set up a series of Accountability Emails that walk through, chapter-by-chapter, theme-by-theme, the material you include in your book.

- **Checklists:** I once created a "10 Steps to Get Your First Client" checklist, which was accompanied by a ten-email series that dug into each step in more detail and continued to reference the checklist PDF. People often end up opting in to a checklist like this when killing time on their phone, whereas they really need it to be printed out from their desktop computer in their home office. By giving subscribers easy access to the checklist PDF *and* methodically walking through each step, new subscribers were much more likely to take the checklist seriously (and later go on to become fantastic customers of mine).

- **Infographics:** These visuals are usually chock full of easy-to-understand statistics. A great infographic makes understanding complex ideas much simpler. But there's really only so much teaching that can be done with a graphic. Think about sending a series of Accountability Emails that draw on the big ideas covered in your infographic, explaining in-depth the implication of each statistic.

– **Cheat sheets:** My friend Amy Hoy created one of the first great lead magnets for a programming framework called Ruby on Rails back in the mid-2000s. Many developers who were trying to understand the framework struggled to know how everything worked "under the hood"—and, let's face it, no one wants to read through stacks of technical documentation. Amy created a simple cheat sheet that helped new Rails developers know the basic functions of the framework, and each function included a simple sentence or two about how it worked and why it mattered. These sorts of cheat sheets are perfectly accompanied by Accountability Sequences that deliver more. In this case, more about what Ruby on Rails is. More about how it's different from other coding frameworks. More about the *why* (whereas the cheat sheet is, most definitely, focused on the *how*).

– **Automated, "evergreen" on-demand webinars:** Many brands are now offering on-demand webinars in exchange for an email address. These are usually sales focused, and are designed to educate, set the stage, and then pitch someone on a product or service at the end. The simple fact is that most attendees will tune it out. Either they won't watch it at all, they'll watch some of it, or they'll be multitasking and only partially paying attention to what's going on. (If Netflix—with shows designed entirely for *entertainment*—can't keep people from mindlessly scrolling through their phone, how do we have any hope with *sales webinars*?) A great Accountability Sequence reinforces the educational tenets that were covered in the webinar and gives people an easy way to get back into the webinar.

- **Email courses:** The next example is all about email courses. Let's look at these more in-depth now . . .

ABOVE AVERAGE

I want your brand to be above average.

Average is what most brands end up doing. Someone ends up on their email list somehow—either by explicitly opting in or, more likely, because they purchased or signed up for something (like an event). The brand then sees fit to shove *everyone* into their "marketing" segment, which means new contacts are soon being badgered with update emails, sales promotions, and whatever else is being blasted to their list.

An above-average brand cares a lot about experience. The easy thing to do is to just hammer everyone with the same communication. It's harder to create better experiences because that requires more content to be created (like the welcome sequences I've outlined in this chapter). But if you want people to stick around and buy, if you want people to tell their friends about your brand, if you want a highly engaged audience—remember the story of the two churches. One was dying; the other was thriving. The growing church put a lot of effort into experience. They didn't just throw new visitors headfirst into their Sunday services; they *onboarded* them into what they believe, who they are, and how they do things differently. This established a foundational baseline that covered both the order and content of each Sunday service.

The ultimate goal of the megachurch was to "save" people. It wasn't enough to just make new people feel welcome by pairing them up with neighborhood leaders. They had to turn sinners into saints. To do this right, their onboarding had to be much more substantial than a simple brand overview: "Here's who we are, here's how we do things, here are some new people you can now call friends." Their onboarding needed to also contain a persuasive overview of the tenets of the faith. They needed new people to crave what they offered. To don my marketing hat again, *they had to create customers.*

In the next chapter we'll take this concept of acclimating new people to your brand and supercharge it. We're going to look at the concept of *creating customers.* How do you take someone who has a particular set of beliefs about something (whether that be Christianity, or the world that you operate in) and condition them to be receptive to what you have to offer? What does it take to establish desire? How do you turn someone who might not really fully appreciate or know that they need what you have to offer and make that continuity between wants and needs a no-brainer?

Let's find out.

Chapter 6

CREATING CUSTOMERS

If you were to survey just about any professional and ask them about the whys and the hows of getting customers, without fail their response would almost always be some variation of, "Because they needed someone like me."

For the longest time, I believed the same. When I first started my software development agency, my understanding was that I had to talk about how we built software, what specific skills we had, and so on. This was my marketing strategy. From there the customers we needed—companies that needed software built—would find us and, with hope, turn into clients.

This did work. We were able to keep the lights on and slowly grow the business. But we were always seemingly one client away from collapse. To get us bigger and better clients, I made a point of going to as many local networking events as I could to meet fellow business owners. My hope was that I'd stumble my way into a conversation that led to me talking about my business, they'd exclaim that they've been searching for a software agency to hire, and we'd end the discussion with a handshake agreement and meeting in the books. An entrepreneurial man can dream, right?

I talked to plenty of business owners and decision makers. Many of them fit the profile of potential clients, but they just weren't looking to hire anyone like us anytime soon. "Shouldn't being forcibly stuck in a room to mingle with fellow business owners be enough?" I thought. "It's like fishing . . . right? Eventually one will bite." It wasn't until I ended up hiring a business coach who had been in the "network marketing" game for decades that I became aware of why my efforts were yielding so little fruit.

The problem, I learned, was that the pool of potential clients who were actively looking for a provider like me is actually pretty low. When people have needs, they reason out or research a solution, weigh the importance and priority of said solution, and then look for someone or something that can satisfy the need. The overall likelihood that the perfect would-be client would be in the same room as me, strike up a conversation with me, and turn into a proper sales meeting later was ridiculously low. This carries over to how many companies do email marketing. Many brands take a "shotgun" approach to sales emails. Send enough stuff, promote enough things, and you'll get sales. What I was missing when finding clients for my agency, and what many brands disregard when selling over email, is the importance of *creating customers*.

Take, for example, the underlying process that had to happen for my agency to get a new client:

- A company had to experience a problem that was holding them back in some way. Sometimes these problems are slow to develop, and at other times they're immediately made clear ("our entire customer database has been hacked!").

- This problem needed to be deemed solvable. Is this just part and parcel of doing business, or can something be done about it?

- Then the problem needed to be sufficiently prioritized. Every company has a list of things they'd like to get done, but unless this problem is particularly important, it might be shelved for later (or never).

- Now the company needed to figure out how to solve this problem. Problems often have several solutions, which can lead down a diverse assortment of paths.

- Next, the company needed to settle on a specific solution and figure out how it could be reached. Can it be done in-house? Is there an off-the-shelf tool that can make this straightforward? Or do we need to look to hire an outside consultant or agency?

- Should they decide on hiring an agency, they'd look around for options. They search the web, ask for recommendations on LinkedIn, or put out a Request for Proposal (RFP).

- If I'm lucky, my company would be somewhere in those search results, or I would serendipitously run into whoever was doing the searching at a random networking mixer.

My agency only hypothetically enters the picture in that last bullet point. Should this company decide to not recognize the problem, not deem it solvable, dismiss its importance, or go in a different direction during any of the above stages, then I've lost the project before I'm even aware of it.

Imagine a direct-to-consumer brand that sells urban wear online. This company has bold growth goals, but they just aren't making enough sales to afford expansion. They've seen how well their competitors are doing and know that they can do better. They're just not sure what they need to do. Increasing online sales is their primary goal, because until that happens, they're not able to grow the business, and they don't have the money to develop additional products.

What's the cause? Well, an all-hands meeting is convened and plenty of options are discussed. The CMO believes it has to do with the ad campaigns. There just aren't enough eyeballs looking at their website. If only more people were aware of their brand, more would buy. Simple.

"Not so fast," counters the head of analytics. The conversion rate from visitors to new sales is super low. While they could spend more money on ads (that they really don't have, he reminds the room), the website is like a leaky faucet. People are flowing in, but almost everyone is leaking out of the funnel.

"It's our messaging," states one of the senior marketers with bravado. The language on the website just isn't persuasive. The calls to action aren't very compelling.

"Don't you think our website is . . . dated?" The art director, who usually focuses just on the design of the clothing, points out that the website doesn't do a good job at reflecting the brand. Their competition has prettier websites, and they're doing better. Surely that's the real problem here.

"Our checkout flow is horrible," contributes their lead programmer. She explains that for someone to buy, they need to fill out a bunch of unnecessary form fields. "Amazon has one-click purchases." A report is quickly generated that shows that there's a high drop-off between adding to cart and purchasing.

There are a lot of possible fixes. And only some of them could end up bringing them to our doorstep. This confusion can often lead to decision paralysis or opting for "kitchen sink" solutions that promise the world. But let's stay optimistic and assume that the team does decide on something my team can help with, like the design of the website. No one on staff has the skill or the bandwidth to take on a full website redesign, so the company starts to look around. If I'm lucky, they'll knock at my door.

Sitting back and waiting for people to know they need what you offer is an ugly way to grow a business. Additionally, the very nature of what played out above means that when a potential client does come knocking, they're almost inevitably knocking on plenty of other doors also. My agency will be seen as simply a provider of services, and considering that there are other providers who seemingly all offer the same services in the running, we'll probably need to compete on price, quality, and speed.

The alternative is to create customers from nothing. Rather than seeking out companies who are looking to redesign their website, you instead target companies that sell things on their website. This is your target audience. Now you think through how you can meet them where they are today and offer them something irresistible. A safe bet for an agency that specializes in web design could be a guide or some other freebie that covers ten ways for direct-to-consumer companies to boost website sales. (A bit like catnip for a DTC company, isn't it?)

Now you focus on helping them identify how they're doing, ideally by providing benchmarks and case studies from wildly successful DTC companies. You deliver a tremendous amount of valuable content that empowers them to understand how to grow their business.

You get them to realize the importance of increasing online sales by highlighting the opportunity cost: *with every day that passes, you're missing out on sales.* You guide them through their options and begin to establish your team and the services you provide as the "fix"—the bridge that's going to lead them to the promised land of abundant online sales.

What's happening here is that you're meeting them where they are today and guiding them. You're the sensei; they're the Karate Kid. You're amplifying the likelihood that they get through the funnel I described above without falling to the wayside. By helping them see what they are missing, there's a strong chance they're going to want to buy from you (and you alone).

Doing this changed the trajectory of my agency. Before, we were sitting back and relying a bit too much on luck. After focusing on creating customers, our marketing objective was to get as many companies as possible into our audience who fit the profile of a company who *might* one day work with us. This was slow-release marketing. It often took months, or even years, to sufficiently prepare someone to be our next client. But we weren't just *vendors*; we were trusted guides for our clients. We no longer had to worry about the competition because our competition was *us*.

With what's possible with email marketing and automation, creating customers can largely be done on autopilot, too. Let's now look at how this is done.

HOW TO CREATE CUSTOMERS: THE L.B.P.S.

Every day, hundreds of new people join your email list. You uncover a wealth of information about each new subscriber that allows you to personalize your content, but you also collect "voice-of-customer" language for your subscribers—giving you all the raw material your brand needs to write highly effective sales copy. These new subscribers are sent a curated series of educational content that establishes, or further reinforces, the problem that your product or service solves. Then they're given a choice: Do you want to attempt to solve this problem on your own, or do you want our help? Many will decide to buy from you right then and there, giving you predictable revenue generated directly from new subscribers. Those who don't buy are then asked what kept them from purchasing and are then segmented based on their objection.

The above example is a completely automated system for onboarding new subscribers, indoctrinating them into your brand, making it clear why they need what you offer, and then automatically pitching them on your products or services. I call it the L.B.P.S. System, and that stands for Lessons-Bridge-Pitch-Survey. This has been used successfully by hundreds of brands to make their email marketing— especially when it comes to getting new subscribers to buy—more predictable and hands-off.

This system, once created, serves as an asset for your business. It's something that you can use as the primary first step for most new people who are exposed to your brand, whether it be because of ads you run, mentions on social media, or calls to action you include in videos, podcasts, or guest posts. Unlike the earlier examples, the L.B.P.S. is designed to sell. And this sale happens within a pretty defined window, usually within two to three weeks of joining your email list. This is important because getting subscribers generally isn't free. Your team is doing the work to market your brand and your L.B.P.S., and you're likely spending money on advertising. If you can recover and, ideally, profit off the cost of acquisition, it means you can pay off the ad spend that led to a new subscriber *before the credit card bill is due at the end of the month*. Think about that for a second. If you're able to drive people not to your paid products, but instead to something free and educational that's also designed to sell, you're going to not only end up with a highly engaged new brand advocate, *but* their admission cost is paid off before you need to pay the AmEx bill!

Before getting into the details of the structure of the L.B.P.S., here's a big-picture overview of what this looks like in action:

1. Lessons
   - A focused **call-to-action is shown**—i.e., the *Ripped-Body Nutrition Setup Guide*—it promises to help someone know exactly what to eat so they can "look better naked."
   - After entering in a first name and email address, a new subscriber is brought to a **confirmation page that surveys them** on their fitness and their goals: How active are they? Do they do any sort of strength training? Are they overweight, normal sized, or underweight? Why do they want to change their body?
   - They're delivered a series of **seven focused lessons over email**, each spaced a day apart, that are all about the relationship between nutrition and their specific health and fitness goals.
   - Each lesson **includes a short quiz** that helps the new subscriber apply and internalize what they just learned. This quiz is actually just a web form, so it's also used to progressively profile the subscriber and segment them even further.

2. Bridge
   - By the end of the crash course, someone **now understands** how important macronutrients are. They know how their fitness goals are directly linked to their nutrition, and nutrition is much more than just total calorie count.
   - A **summary "cheat sheet" PDF** is sent a few days after the final lesson that sums everything up, and hints that next week a special offer will be available for the comprehensive book, *The Diet Adjustments Manual*.
   - Later that week, an email with the subject "Readers who crushed it" goes out. This catalogs the transformation stories of a bunch of people like the new subscriber. It's **designed to overcome any self-doubts that might accompany the educational content** that was delivered over the last few days. The email closes by reinforcing next week's special offer, and quickly highlights how it differs from the free course.

3. Pitch
   - A five-day **personal promotion window** for the *Diet Adjustment Manual* opens up on Monday. The subscriber is presented with two options: either do a bunch of dubious internet searching to come up with the recipes, nutrition information, and more they will need to really fix their nutrition . . . or take the "shortcut" and let the *Manual* lay out the exact step-by-step framework they need.
   - **Urgency is created** by offering a limited-time discount for the *Manual*. In the next chapter on pitching, we'll cover urgency tactics more in-depth.

- The **usual pitch tactics are used:** strong case studies, before-and-after examples, FAQs, and other information that highlights the risk of "figuring it out yourself." This will also be covered in depth in the next chapter.
4. Survey
   - The week after the personal promotion window, a **simple survey is sent out to non-buyers**. This survey uncovers what held someone back from buying.
   - Depending on how someone answers, they're then **segmented** based on their primary objection to purchasing and optionally **re-pitched** immediately or at a future date with a focus on overcoming that objection.

Yes, there's quite a bit going on in an L.B.P.S., but I know that once you take the time to create this asset it'll be one of the most predictably lucrative systems you have for turning prospects into buyers.

Lessons

A good course, whether free or paid, should do more than just deliver knowledge. It needs to transform. And it needs to be focused on meeting someone where they (collectively) are today and guide them to where they need to be next.

The course you'll be developing is no different, but in this case is designed with one single task in mind: *to create new customers*. What you don't want to have happen is to put someone in front of a product or service of yours and have them simultaneously *learn* why they need it, and then *decide* that you're who they should buy from. Educating *and* selling rarely works, so you're going to want to make sure that the

114

material you include in your course is singularly focused on establishing the problem and showing that it can be solved.

This course is going to make it obvious that a problem exists. *Here is the problem, and here's what happens when it goes unsolved.* Ideally this is dependent on how someone initially segmented themselves— for example, why do they want to get properly fit? (For example, maybe they're self-conscious, or maybe they're just tired of feeling tired and in pain.)

Once you've highlighted the problem, you then need to make it obvious that this problem can be solved—and make it clear what this solution looks like. This might seem a bit obvious at first, but not everyone is consciously mindful of the fact that there is an alternative. That the problem that's been brought to light can be eliminated.

And, finally, you need to offer some ideas around *how* someone can solve the problem. Most problems have multiple solutions, and the product or service you ultimately want them to buy is likely just one of a few different options. By equipping someone with the know-how to self-assess and solve their problems, you're empowering them to be an *incredible* customer of yours. Why? Because when you do pitch them, you won't be forcing them into a corner and shouting, "Surprise! It's time to buy!" Rather, you'll have made a clear case for what's at stake, how it can be solved, ways it can be solved, and why you offer the best, most economic, most reliable, and most desirable means for fixing their problem.

Imagine that you're out for a walk, and it suddenly starts to pour. It's pretty cold out, so it's not one of those glorious tropical rains— rather, it's a wet, bone-chilling downpour. The **problem** is that you're now wet, cold, and really uncomfortable. The **solution** is simply the inverse of the problem. You're now dry, warm, and comfortable. The "**fix**," or the products/offers that can bring someone from a problem to fully realize a solution, or to at least get closer to it, can include a number of different things:

- **An umbrella:** This will stop you from getting even more wet, but you'll still be shivering. You're a bit closer to the solution, and might even dry off after a while, but you're not totally warm or comfortable.
- **A towel and a change of clothes:** You go inside, dry off, and put some new clothes on. You're dry and slowly getting more comfortable. This eventually leads to the solution you're after.
- **A hot bath, a luxurious robe, and a plush sofa by a roaring fire:** Now we're talking. You go inside, dip into a hot bath, and then sit by the fire in a soft cotton robe. You've gone above and beyond the solution. Not only are you dry, warm, and comfortable—you're feeling *great*.

Can you see how the first option somewhat reaches the intended solution, the second satisfies it, and the third surpasses it? This is exactly the sort of thing you want to bake into your educational lessons. You want your paid product or service to be the thing they ultimately want, but you need to give them other "outs." You want to show them that there are other methods of somewhat or totally reaching the solution they're looking for, but yours just happens to be the best.

Another less immediately obvious but *incredibly* important benefit to this sort of educational asset is that you can use it to market to people who aren't actually looking for a company like yours, and possibly don't even think that they need what you offer. Take, for example, a garden design company. Not every homeowner thinks they need to ever hire a garden designer for their backyard. Many probably think it's something exclusively for the rich.

The garden design company could create an L.B.P.S. dedicated to helping people transform their backyard into the ultimate space for parties, backyard BBQs, and other social gatherings. It could find out a bit about each subscriber (Do they have kids? Pets? How big is their yard?) and then use that to deliver a crash course on how to plan the ultimate backyard, decide on vegetation, plan an outdoor kitchen, and more. The goal would be to help turn the average homeowner into someone who knows just enough about garden design and layout, all the while realizing that doing it *right* is a big investment and . . . well, they don't want to screw it up. This L.B.P.S. would equip someone with a basic framework for designing their own backyard, but it would also make it clear that there's a lot of risk in doing it wrong.

The pitch is pretty simple. You can either:

- Do nothing and keep your backyard as is.
- Go and buy a bunch of gardening and landscaping books, spend a lot of time getting more familiar with garden design, and then have a go at designing the ultimate backyard, coming up with a supply list, and installing it.
- Have our team of experts do it all for you.

Those who want it done right and have the money to spend will probably go for the latter option, which means the L.B.P.S. has turned a free subscriber into a paying customer. And while the majority won't buy but will either attempt to go at it on their own or (more likely) just do nothing, they'll continue to appreciate the help the garden design company has given them already. As subscribers to their email list, they'll also continue getting future helpful and educational content sent to them. Over time, quite a few of these subscribers who may not have hired the company during the L.B.P.S. will come back and hire them months or years later.

A paid ad campaign for a garden design company is really only going to appeal to homeowners who have been thinking about hiring a designer to help with their backyard. But a free course on creating the ultimate backyard? Every homeowner wants that. This is the power of a great L.B.P.S. It's going to *create customers* from a pool of people who fit the profile of the sort of people who buy from you but might not yet be problem-aware enough to know that they need you.

How long your course is, both in individual lesson length and the number of lessons you deliver, doesn't really matter. Most of the email courses I've seen tend to have between seven and nine lessons, and average around one thousand words apiece. This means every lesson is easy enough to read in one sitting, and probably doesn't cover so much that it overwhelms the reader. And at seven to nine total lessons, spaced a day apart, you'll end up becoming a mainstay in their inbox for a week. And rather than associating your brand with just trying to sell them stuff, instead you're showing up every day with something legitimately helpful—and all you're asking from them, at least for now, is for a bit of time and attention.

Taking Action

A common mistake with educational email courses is to have them be read-only. People get your daily email, read it, and then move on to whatever's next. While there will undoubtedly be some subscribers who figure out how to take what you're teaching and apply it, the single best thing you can do for engagement and overall subscriber success is to encourage your readers to act on what you're teaching them.

The way to do this is to include quizzes or worksheets with every lesson you send. These should, ideally, be links to online forms that provide a mixture of "choose one of many" lists and free-form text input fields. What you want is to help someone really think through what you've covered and find ways that it applies to them and their situation.

Here's an example from an L.B.P.S.:

> . . . So chew on these ideas for a bit. Think about how it is you present yourself to your clients. Are you pitching yourself as an employee-without-benefits who provides commodity design services? And if you are, how are you going to ever be able to break free of how the market prices your commodity service?
>
> This is why most freelancers are underpaid. They're caught in a race to the bottom and they're selling and pitching the same stuff as everyone else.
>
> Today's worksheet is short, but it'll help you think about how your clients perceive you now:
>
> **Worksheet: How Do You Present Yourself to Clients?**
>
> Once you fill out the worksheet, I'll send you a copy of your answers and I'll also get a copy. I'll also then send you Lesson 3.

When the worksheet link is clicked, a simple web form is shown that asks for people to answer three questions:

- *"How have you historically determined what to charge?"* (Options: "I'd use a free online rate or project calculator or research what others are charging," "I'd calculate the effective hourly rate of my last job," "I'd just pick a number and hope it works.")
- *"How have you described yourself to prospective clients?"* (Free-form text.)
- *"Do you think the way you've described yourself has negatively affected you in the past?"* (Free-form text.)

This worksheet alone has had over seven thousand submissions since 2016, and has resulted in raw feedback like:

"Typically, I describe myself as a freelance writer. I'll highlight some of my background or experience that I think fits with the client's needs, but, on-the-whole, I almost always say 'I'm a freelancer.'"

And:

"It's caused their eyes to glaze over as they don't know what I'm talking about . . . 'What's a sales funnel?' Also, I'm too cheap. Lost a potential client last week because he said, 'Why are your fees so low, you can't be any good for that rate . . . do you know what's involved in this project?' and he went to someone else instead who was charging 100s per month more for the 'same thing.'"

This is a research gold mine. Every day, people provide high-quality voice-of-customer data that describes how they've personally struggled with the ideas taught in the course. And over time, macro-trends are able to be extracted—the same problems are faced, the same excuses are made, and so on. All of this can then be used to create the ultimate sales pitches that are based not on the ideas of some outsourced copywriter, but the actual *described* pain points from those in the target audience.

The Intro and the Outro

While your email course should prepare someone to be a customer, it should also prepare someone to be a customer of a *specific* product or service you offer. The end goal of your L.B.P.S. is to successfully pitch someone on an offer, so what you teach should obviously closely align to what you pitch. (If you're trying to sell golf gear, an email course on parenting wouldn't make much sense, would it?)

When someone joins your L.B.P.S., you're going to be collecting *why* segmentation that reflects the primary challenge they need your help with. But you should also provide a very specific ask at the end of the first lesson email you send:

> —Brennan
> Co-founder, RightMessage
> P.S. I really appreciate that you're going through this new course of ours. Would you mind taking about thirty seconds to reply to this email and share what you expect to learn from this course? This will help us ensure that we've created the *right* course—thanks!

You're trying to do two things here:

1. **Track whether expectations align with reality.** Is the course you're teaching what people are expecting of you? If you're consistently getting feedback that doesn't align with

what you're actually teaching, it might be time to revisit your lessons.

2. **Get even more engagement with your audience.** You're making it clear that there's a human (or team of humans) waiting to hear from them. By asking this simple question, you're making it obvious that you care.

As an added bonus, email providers regard replies to email as something "natural." When you get an email from your boss, a colleague, a partner, or a friend, you generally reply to it. Emails that get replies send a strong signal that this is a reputable sender, which ultimately ends up boosting your deliverability score. The higher your brand's deliverability score, the more likely your emails are to stay out of people's spam folders.

When you deliver your final lesson, you should have another ask at the footer of your email. This one finds out whether what you taught aligned with what they were expecting:

—Brennan
Co-Founder, RightMessage
P.S. Thanks for completing the course! Next week, I'll be sending you an email that summarizes everything you've learned and includes a handy cheat sheet that you can reference in the future.
If you don't mind: Could you let me know what you thought of this mini-course, and whether it lined up with what you were expecting? My team and I are always tweaking what we teach, and we want to make sure you're fully satisfied with what we sent you. Thanks in advance!

Not only will this help ensure that you're teaching the right material *after* someone's gone through your course, but it's a fantastic way to get testimonials on autopilot. People will write back with mostly positive reviews of what you've sent, and you'll be able to take this feedback and (with permission) turn it into testimonials that you can use to further promote your L.B.P.S.

Bridge

After you've delivered your final lesson, you're going to want to wait a few days and then send what's called the Bridge Sequence.

A mistake I made early on was to jump straight from educational content into a sales page. Having met with many marketers over the years, this is a common pitfall that many of us have learned really doesn't work. Sure, you'll get sales—but you won't get nearly as many as you should. How come? Once again, it's all about expectations.

If you're on the receiving end of a great course on garden design for the typical suburban homeowner, and then a day or two after the course wraps up, you're hit hard with "hire us!" emails, that's probably going to leave a bad taste. Even though you know the course creators aren't a charity, and run a garden design business, you're caught blindsided by their paid offering. You're not against it, but you are surprised by it.

Once you've done the groundwork of creating a new customer and making it crystal clear what the problem is, how it can be solved, and why it needs to be eliminated, you need to hand it over to your *subscribers* to take that next step. A sales pitch is, by definition, pressure. You're telling someone they should buy from you. But with a Bridge, you're handing the reins over to them.

Long before I was involved in business and marketing, I was a student at a small liberal arts college. I was studying classical literature and philosophy, with a focus on the Greeks. This meant I ended up reading a lot of Plato, a student of Socrates whose *Dialogues* featured Socrates going around ancient Athens and conversing with its citizens.

What was interesting about Socrates's approach, which all of us would do well to internalize—especially those of us who engage in Facebook arguments—was that he realized just how difficult it is to change someone's opinion. You couldn't expect to just tell someone they're wrong and have them change their mind on the spot. Yet Socrates had an agenda. He wanted the people he talked with to believe a certain set of truths.

So what did Socrates do? He asked the right questions. By meeting people where they were, he was able to get *them* to admit certain things about reality—and to uncover for themselves inherent contradictions or fallacies. This questioning would eventually lead to the truth he wanted them to arrive at. And ultimately, he was able to get people to have an epiphany, and a new way of looking at reality, *which aligned perfectly with the reality he had in mind from the outset.*

Socrates considered himself to be a "philosophical midwife." He wasn't a teacher of philosophy or a peddler of philosophical truths. Rather, he knew that he was there to help people along. To move from the World of Today to the World of Tomorrow.

Consider the following excerpt, from Plato's *Theaetetus*:

Socrates: I am like the midwife, in that I cannot myself give birth to wisdom. The common reproach is true, that, though I question others, I can myself bring nothing to light because there is no wisdom in me . . . Of myself I have no sort of wisdom, nor has any discovery ever been born to me as the child of my soul. Those who frequent my company at first appear, some of them, quite unintelligent, but, as we go further with our discussions, [some] make progress at a rate that seems surprising to others as well as to themselves, although it is clear that they have never learned anything from me. The many admirable truths which they bring to birth have been discovered by themselves from within . . .

The proof of this is that many who have not been conscious of my assistance but have made light of me, thinking it was all their own doing, have left me sooner than they should . . . and then suffered miscarriage of their thoughts through falling into bad company. They lost the children of whom I had delivered them by bringing them up badly, caring more for false phantoms than for the true . . .

Those who seek my company have the same experience as a woman giving birth. They suffer labor pains and by night and day are full of distress. My art has power to bring on these pains or alleviate them.[11]

You might be questioning what any of this has to do with this Bridge Sequence. Well, it has a lot to do with it. Because what we want is to posit a few future realities for our subscribers, with our paid product or service positioned as one of these realities.

After someone learns something new from you, and ends up with a new awareness and appreciation for a specific problem they're afflicted by and its ability to be solved, there are three possible paths you want to show them:

- **Do nothing.** Continue being afflicted by the problem and suffering all the side effects and limitations that accompany it.
- **Figure it out yourself.** Take the kernel of knowledge we delivered over the last few days and run with it. Continue doing your own research. Try it yourself. Look for another product or service that you think might be able to fully deliver on solving said problem. But know it's risky. The path is arduous and full of dangers. And the cost to backtrack, admit defeat, and do it right is great.
- **Let us be your guide.** We've shown that we know our stuff. You've benefited already from us (what you've learned from our course has outweighed the time you've invested). You've seen examples of how we've helped others solve this problem. We can get you from A to B effectively and with minimal risk.

The Product as the Guide

Your product isn't just something you're trying to get someone to buy; it's the barge that's going to carry them from the World of Today to the World of Tomorrow. When the would-be customer perceives what you have to offer this way, their entire perception changes. You're not just a vendor—you're a partner. You don't just have a product to offer—you have a shortcut to tomorrow.

Your subscribers need to see the three options above as:

- **Failure:** You don't actually have any desire to solve your problem.
- **Risk:** You could, but you're probably going to scrape your knees a bunch in the process (translation: hire the wrong competing product, make silly and costly financial mistakes,

spend way too much time thinking about this stuff when you have, for example, a business to run!).

- **Security:** This brand knows what they're doing, they've already provided me with a lot to think about, they're giving, they're experts, and they have the solution to my exact problem.

Now it's not about buying or not buying. Instead, the subscriber weighs: *Do I give up? Do I gamble? Or do I take the safe bet?* You want the kind of customers and clients who decide on the latter option.

The Two Emails You'll Send

Now that you have the playbook, let's get tactical. Your Bridge should be two emails and serve to provide a buffer week between when you wrap up your lessons and when the subscriber's personal pitch window opens up. These emails are designed to bridge together the free with the paid. The first email will summarize what they've learned already in the free course, and the second will serve to set the stage for your paid product or service.

Email #1: The Summary (sent Tuesday)

The first email's job is to summarize everything that was covered in your lessons. It should drive home exactly what someone has learned, ideally condensed into neatly formatted bullet points. You want to make a strong case here for how much value you've dumped on this subscriber—don't make them come to that realization on their own; tell them!

This email also needs to bring up the "what's next" question. Is it stagnation (do nothing), risk (do-it-yourself), or security (we give you exactly what you need)? Without being too overt, you want to make it obvious that implementing or realizing everything you've covered in your free course is their next step. Simply learning about a problem and how to solve it is totally useless if the problem persists. Make it clear that you have a safe solution to their problem.

Finally, you're going to want to close this first email by hinting at what's coming next week: a personal sales window for *exactly* the product or service they need from you. You want them to know it's coming, and you want to start getting them excited. And, in closing, have them keep an eye out for another email from you later in the week that goes into a bit more detail.

Email #2: Crossing the Divide (sent Thursday)

This email is designed to preemptively overcome any objections some-one might have *before* being presented with your product or service. You've already made a strong case for the problem your paid offering solves, and the necessity of solving it. But depending on either how expensive your product is *or* how much time and mental energy it'll require of them, people are going to be . . . people. They're going to erect roadblocks. They're going to make excuses for why they can't do this, and why they should just keep doing what they've been doing.

What you want this email to do is to really tie everything together. "You know what needs to be done, you know some ways of doing it, now you need to *know* that you can actually pull this off. And we want you to know that we have your back."

Here's an example of a Crossing the Divide email that I use in one of my L.B.P.S. sequences (this example is specifically targeting those who said their *why* is that they're writing, sending, and losing proposal after proposal):

Tens of thousands of freelancers have gone through my free email course so far—and while I've gotten thousands of worksheet submissions and replies from students, it's been interesting what I learned AFTER I started surveying people . . .

Most people don't end up doing anything (like setting up a proper system for actually writing and winning proposals) after going through this course!!!

After a lot of surveying and phone calls, I learned that the reason had little to do with the instruction. And in most cases, students knew what they were doing wrong and what they'd need to start doing in the future.

The big issue for most was **"imposter syndrome"**— the internal fear that comes with taking ownership over how and what you're selling.

For example, take how you price yourself:

When you're pricing yourself as a commodity and going along with the market rate of whatever it is you do, it's easy to justify your costs. You just point to other people like you. I call it "me-too pricing."

But breaking free of that fear doesn't come easy to most.

It didn't come easy to me. I'm an introvert. Looking at a client in the eye and telling them that I charge $25,000+ a week to write email copy and tweak their website doesn't come easy.

But because I'm confident about what I price and am very comfortable at Socratically questioning prospective clients and gauging the value of their projects, I'm able to confidently sell and quote projects.

However, that's just me, the guy who teaches this course—I'm not you, and you and I probably don't do the same work, have the same kind of clients, and so on.

So as a way of inspiring you to charge what you're worth, I want to give you some case studies from a handful of my students who are absolutely crushing it. They're charging more, delivering better work to their clients, and experiencing all the fruits of better rates (easier to close deals, more time to spend with their family/friends, more creative flexibility).

Check the following success stories out—which of these stories resonates best with you?

- Maya has gone from $38k/yr to $100k this year (and she's just 24)
- Bart has grown his business to 13 employees w/ ~20 active projects at a time
- Torre went from $35 an hour to $2,000 a week
- Ciprian is able to finally invest in his business and in his life since he's raised his rates by 250 percent
- Drew is on track to hitting $500k in revenue this year
- Jim has learned how to masterfully qualify and sell his project leads
- Matt has doubled his site's traffic and is now closing five-figure projects (where before he was selling $3–5k gigs)
- Kai has 5x'ed his rate and his business is growing like a weed

All of the people above have been able to substantially raise their prices. And as you read in the stories above, many of them had doubts and inhibitions that they could do this. Many almost failed before they even began.

I've now taught you the strategy . . .

You know why you shouldn't call yourself a freelancer.

You know that you need to position yourself as an investment.

You now know the power of anchoring your prices against the pay-off of the project.

While knowing the strategy is often enough to "win the war," it's much easier when you're equipped with the tactics, tools, and personal accountability you need to become a success story like the ones I listed above.

So here's what's happening next Tuesday:

My online course, *Double Your Freelancing Rate* (DYFR), which has equipped more than 8,000 people with the know-how and specific tools they need to raise their rates, is currently available on my website.

Next week, I'm putting together a special offer for you—and it's only available for three days . . .

You're not going to want to miss this—especially if you're ready to seriously double down on the foundations I've already taught in this email course.

I'll send you all the details to grab this offer on Tuesday.

If the following are true for you . . . I'd highly recommend you keep an eye out for next week's email from me 😃 .

- You got a lot of value out of this free course and see that you've made mistakes in how you've positioned and presented yourself in the past.
- You're interested in a more systematic, immersive course that will help you with qualifying, learning about, and pitching clients at a substantially higher price.
- You want the exact email templates and word-for-word scripts that I and hundreds of successful students of mine use when selling.
- You want the legal documents (contract, statement of work, retainer) and proposal template my students and I use to close sales.
- You want personal accountability and support from me and thousands of other students in our private, students-only forum.

Get ready for next week. It's time to arm yourself with the instruction, tools, and accountability you need to guarantee a better freelancing income.

Have a great rest of your week and talk to you soon.

—Brennan

And here's how Andy Morgan of RippedBody,[12] a fitness coach and author, uses this email to instill confidence after sending their crash course on nutrition:

Tens of thousands of frustrated trainees have taken my free email course. It's been fascinating what I learned after I started surveying people.

Strangely, most still didn't end up tweaking their diets based on their progress data.

This was weird. So I started asking why.

I learned that the reason had little to do with the instruction. In most cases, the issue was that they didn't have the confidence to make decisions. They felt they were constantly **"second-guessing"** themselves.

For example, let's say your weight loss has stopped, and you reduced your carb and fat intake to reduce your caloric intake by 200 each day.

☞ A little extra hunger is kicking in,
☞ Your stomach measurements still aren't dropping, and
☞ Your last training session felt off.

You're now worried—have you *done the right thing?* 😫

This is natural. You don't have the same level of experience I do. Hell, when I first started working with people, I wasn't sure sometimes whether I was making the right decisions either!

So as a way of inspiring you, I want to give you some case studies. These are all formerly frustrated readers who became clients.

The common thread?

They said the key to breaking through their plateau was that hiring me forced them to start tracking their progress because all the decisions could then flow from that.

JOHN

John lost 46 lbs . . .

John lost 46 lbs and set himself free from his cycle of program (and coach) hopping that led him nowhere.

CAMERON

Cameron broke through his plateau . . .

Cameron lost 100 lbs, then got stuck and didn't know what to do (left). He broke through his plateau to build himself a physique that [is] . . . well, I think quite enviable!

(The loose skin is unavoidable when you lose nearly half your body weight.)

CHANDLER

Chandler broke free of his skinny-fat purgatory . . .

Chandler broke free of his skinny-fat purgatory and gained 13 lbs of muscle (which looks more like 20).

TARIQ

Tariq was scared that he'd look skinny . . .

Tariq was scared that he'd look skinny if he lost any more fat but felt too fat to bulk. 19 lbs later, I'll let you be the judge of whether that's the case.

STUART

Stuart, after spending his life as a frustrated trainee . . .

Stuart was 39 and had spent his life a frustrated trainee. He built himself into a beast in just a few short years.

All of the people above were able to take their physiques to a level they didn't think was possible.

It brings me great joy coaching people, but there is just one of me and I can't work with everyone who applies to work with me.

So, in 2015 I decided to take a break from coaching and live off my savings.

I wanted to figure out how I could teach people to have the same level of success that coaching can bring, but at a fraction of the cost and without my time being the bottleneck.

It took me 6 months before I figured it out, but the resulting idea was to document my decision-making processes into a system.

The result was a book and video package called 📖 *The Diet Adjustments Manual.* It's now on the third edition, which was released in April 2021.

Next week, I'm putting together a special offer for you—and it's only available for three days . . .

My book and video package, *The Diet Adjustments Manual*, which has equipped more than 4,300 people with the know-how, specific tools, and examples they need to start making progress, is currently available on my website.

From Tuesday I'm going to make it available to you for 50 percent off.

If any of the following are true for you, I'd highly recommend you keep an eye out for next week's email.

👉 You've seen from the course the mistakes you've made in the past.

> ☞ You're ready to double down on the foundations I've already taught.
>
> ☞ You're interested in learning a more systematic method for evaluating your progress so that you can have confidence in your decisions and avoid long plateaus.
>
> ☞ You want to see real client examples of the decisions I made as I coached them so that you can act with confidence and see how it applies to yourself.
>
> If this sounds appealing, get ready for next week. I've got you covered.
>
> Talk to you soon. 😊
>
> —Andy

Pitch

You've now truly created a customer. You've helped someone understand a problem that's holding them back, explained why it's so important to solve this problem, helped them see past their own internal fears or doubts, and self-equipped your new subscriber with a few ideas on how to get to the World of Tomorrow. Additionally, you've made it clear that you have a "shortcut" to get them there, and that you're putting together a special offer for them that kicks off in a few days.

Now it's time to actually make them an offer. It's time for you to get paid.

The first time I really experienced the power of educate-first, sell-later was when I was running my web agency in the mid-2000s. Our team regularly hosted free workshops and networking mixers out of our office. We'd invite the local business community to come learn about what the differences were between iPhone and Android apps, what to do when you're overwhelmed by emailing Excel files around the office, and more. We'd also go over to organizations, like our local chamber of commerce, and host the same workshops. We ended up with quite a few regulars who would come out to all of our events. I remember once getting a call from one of these regulars—a nondescript guy who I'd talked to a few times but I wouldn't say I knew that well. He said he had a project he needed us to build and was eager to get started. We went through the discovery and proposal phase and priced it out at just over $100,000. Within an hour after sending the proposal, he accepted.

That was, by far, the easiest hundred grand I ever made. But we made it because of the cumulation of all the value we'd been delivering over the months he'd been hanging around us. He'd learned a lot from us. He saw that we really knew what we were doing. He showed up to our "Client Launch" parties, where we'd celebrate publicly anytime we handed off a new web app or website to a local client. Simply put, he knew we were legitimate. *That* is how we were able to sell a high-priced project so "easily"—it's because the usual issues around trusting the vendor, trusting whether they should engage in a project like this, all of those doubts, were preemptively squashed in a group, one-to-many format. He'd sat in on our workshops. Overheard the discussions we led. We sold him and dozens of others concurrently, rather than needing to do it one-to-one.

This is exactly what you're doing with everything we've covered above. You're creating systems that do much of the selling automatically. Your team will go in occasionally and test and tweak, but for the most part, the email system you'll be creating doesn't mind if you throw a dozen, a hundred, or ten thousand people at it.

When I quickly closed on this six-figure project, I realized that I wasn't needing to prove our agency in any way. Instead, the bulk of the sales discussion (if you even want to call it that!) was centered around what we'd be building for his company, when we could realistically start, and other details. Likewise, when you pitch subscribers within your L.B.P.S., you're not going to need to really educate them on *why* they need what you're offering—you've already done that. Instead, you need to just focus on how this will get them from today to tomorrow efficiently, economically, and reliably. You want the investment, not the cost, of moving forward with your offer to far outweigh the alternatives, including doing nothing, trying to DIY a solution, or risking it all on a competing, but inferior, company's product.

The Mechanics of the Pitch

The entire next chapter is dedicated to pitching, so I'm not going to duplicate much of what I'll say there. But because this pitch is coming right after you've delivered a Lessons and Bridge Sequence, there are a few nuances we'll want to go over. I also want to include a few examples of L.B.P.S. pitch emails.

The length of your pitch window, and the number of emails, should be contingent on both how expensive and how time intensive what you're offering is. If you're selling something straightforward that's a few hundred dollars or less, you don't need to really exaggerate your sales sequence. A few days, and a few emails, is probably sufficient. But if you're looking to sell someone on hiring a pricey consulting service or a premium multi-thousand-dollar offering, you might need to extend your window.

Here's my rule of thumb when it comes to the duration of an L.B.P.S. pitch window:

- < $100 offer, 2–3 days
- $100–$500 offer, 3–5 days
- $500+ offer, 5–9 days

You've already established the need, so these emails are all designed to help someone work through the *logistics* of what you're offering:

- Is this something I can financially budget for right now?
- What sort of ROI can I realistically expect?
- How does this compare and contrast against other options?
- Do I really need to get all the way to the solution I want (tomorrow)?
- How much time will this require of me, and can I budget that?
- If I need to justify this to others who haven't gone through the L.B.P.S. and don't have the level of awareness I have, how do I do that?

A Complete L.B.P.S. Pitch

Let's look at how the team at RippedBody writes their L.B.P.S. pitch emails:

Email #1 (Monday)

This is a final conditioning email that's sent the day before the promotion window opens up.

Tomorrow, as a thank you for taking my email course, I'll be sending you a personal 50 percent off link to get *The Diet Adjustments Manual 3.0.*

This is your chance to join over 4,300 others.

This will ONLY be open until midnight this Friday. **So if you're thinking of getting it—make sure you check your inbox tomorrow.**

A few quick things to know before tomorrow:

1. It's not just written content. You'll also be getting video screen-shares of me going over actual client data explaining my decisions step-by-step as I coached them.
2. It's backed by a full money-back guarantee. If you don't think what you're getting outweighs the cost, email me, and I'll gladly refund you. I want you to be successful, not just a customer.
3. You'll get future editions free of charge—for life. When I released the third edition at the start of April 2021, all 3,600 people who purchased a previous edition received an updated copy.

Thank you for considering it! 🙏 😊

Some notes on the above, and why I think what they're doing is so smart:

— The email course has been entirely text based. The premium product extends that by providing videos, loads of spreadsheet data, and more.

— They're immediately reversing the risk. Even though they're offering their book at a generous 50 percent–off discount, "if you don't think what you're getting outweighs the cost, email me."

- You're getting in relatively early. As more updates are made, you won't be penalized and need to buy the new version or pay more as others might.

But the real job of this email is this: *To remind someone of what you told them the previous week. Tomorrow a personalized promotion window opens up for the "upsell" to the email course.*

Email #2 (Tuesday)

Hey, the big day is here.

You can get *The Diet Adjustments Manual* for 50 percent off through Friday at midnight. 📖

If you're frustrated with your fat loss efforts, instead of thinking, "I'm doing everything right, why isn't this working?!"

Flip your mindset to, "I'm clearly doing something wrong, and *I'm going to figure this out as plenty of others have before me.*"

If your mind is in the right place, this book, which builds on *The Nutrition Setup Guide*, is your solution.

Equip yourself with the framework, tools, and examples you need to take all the guesswork, anxiety, and complexity out of physique transformation.

The *Diet Adjustments Manual*—Click to buy

People pay hundreds of dollars per month for coaching. This is my nutrition coaching knowledge in a book so that you can do it yourself.

The 50 percent discount is only for the next 3 days.

> **Get your copy for $49 now.** 📖
> If you have any questions, just hit reply and let me know. 🙏
> —Andy

Notice the lack of trust building. There's nothing about who Andy is or who else is on the RippedBody team. The person reading this already knows who Andy & Co. are, and they already know why they need this book.

"If your mind is in the right place, this book, which builds on The Nutrition Setup Guide [the name of the L.B.P.S.], is your solution."

They're leaving it up to the reader here. *Are you ready? If so, this augments and expands on everything you've already learned in our free email course.* Unlike the email course, you'll get the exact "framework, tools, and examples" that will enable you to transform your physique.

Email #3 (Wednesday)

> ☛ You know why calorie balance and your macros are the most important things for fat loss.
> ☛ You know that you need to track so that you have data to base decisions on.
> ☛ And you know that it's the adjustments you make that make the difference between spinning your wheels and being on track with your target.
>
> But to become a success story like the ones I have shared, it's helpful to have a decision-making system.

The long road is to go out and piece together the free information you find on the internet. Through trial and error, you might find what works for you. 😵

I took this journey, and I don't regret it, but it swallowed up a decade before I figured things out for myself. You can take that path if you want, but if your time is worth more than what I'm asking, then I'd suggest the alternative . . .

The shortcut is to use my system, developed through ten years of coaching 1,000+ frustrated trainees like yourself. 🤓

My book and video package, *The Diet Adjustments Manual*, is that system. It will show you precisely what you need to do and when. And this is the third edition, triple the length of the original, built on reader feedback.

The smartest people in the world have had mentors. Look over my shoulder as I explain exactly how I achieve the results I do for my clients so you can replicate that for yourself.

"This is EXACTLY what I have always wanted but never had. I recommend it to friends without hesitation. While your website is great, I find that your manual is so much more in-depth, and I really couldn't be happier with the money I've spent." —Steve Corbett

You don't have to guess your way through this.

Join 4,300 others. Get your copy for $49 (50 percent off). 📱

But remember, the sale ends Friday.

If you have any questions, just hit reply. 🙏

—Andy

I really like the way this email kicks off: "You know why calorie balance and your macros are the most important things for fat loss." (*You know this because I taught you this over the last few days.*)

"You know that you need to track so that you have data to base decisions on." (*You know this because I taught you this.*)

"You know it's the adjustments you make that make the difference between spinning your wheels and being on track with your target." (*We covered this in the sixth lesson of the free course.*)

This pitch is entirely rooted in the fact that someone who's reading it already is on the exact same wavelength as the RippedBody team. There's a shared glossary that's been established. Both sides are in agreement as to what the issue is and how it can be fixed.

Andy's question? "Do you want to become one of the success stories I shared with you earlier? If you do, you need my book."

You'll also notice how there's a constant push-pull between letting RippedBody figure it all out for you vs. "guessing your way through this." Remember what the competition is here. It's someone deciding to do nothing, to DIY it, or to pick up a book or program from another fitness website that might conflict and clash with the new worldview that Andy and his team have instilled in their subscribers.

A few years ago, I remember having dinner with my friend Patrick, who at the time was running a very successful single-person consultancy. He was regularly asked to speak at conferences around the world and was in very high demand as a conversion optimization consultant. The reason he was asked to speak at so many conferences and sought after by so many companies was because he was a prolific educator. His personal blog, Kalzumeus.com, was known for having some of the most in-depth content available on search engine optimization and optimizing for on-site conversions.

Patrick relayed the story of a recent high-value consulting project he was bidding on. The competition was fierce—the main contender was an international consulting conglomerate. They had full-time staff who sat and responded to RFPs (Requests for Proposals) all day and knew exactly what had to be written to guarantee being awarded the contract. They knew what they were doing, they knew how to wine and dine their clients, and they usually didn't find themselves needing to compete with former English teachers living in Japan. But Patrick won the project. And not because of his price or availability or any of the usual subjects. He won because the stakeholder at the company had been following his blog for a while, and their idea of how search engine optimization should be done was identical to Patrick's ideas on the subject. Why the lack of divergence? Because they had learned everything they knew about search optimization from Patrick's blog and email list over the years.

Like Patrick, Andy and his team know the importance of primacy. They have an opinion on how fitness should be done, and they want their audience to have the same opinion. This way, it's never a competition between their book or another book. It's always, even if just subconsciously, "Does this book, this course, or this coach align with what I believe to be true about macronutrients and fitness [which I've taken wholesale for the team at RippedBody]?"

Email #5 (Thursday)

1. **It's a visual treat and easy to understand.**
   We've all read books that we struggled to compre-hend and couldn't recall. This will definitely not be the case with all the visuals I have put in the new book.

   > *"The number of visuals really helps people understand what's going on, what expecta-tions to have, and the numerous examples also help people see what you mean. Well done!"* —Eric Helms

2. **It's comprehensive enough to cover almost any question or detail you may want to know more about.**
   I've run RippedBody.com for 10 years and have answered over 20,000 questions, and trained 2,000+ clients.

   After crushing your first fat loss phase, you aren't going to get stuck not knowing what to do next. Cut, bulk, maintenance, and transition phases are all covered, with long-term planning.

   Here's a 7-minute video I shot explaining the content.

3. **The detailed client result explanations will leave you feeling reassured and less alone.**

4. **It will save you a LOT of time and wasted effort.**

   > *"Clear and concise, easy to follow, informa-tive, and plenty of 'aha!' moments through-out."* —Robert Plant

Don't miss out on finding the "aha!" moments as Robert did, which could save you months of hard work.

5. **There's no risk because I offer a money-back guarantee.**
   If you don't feel like it was worth the price, just email me, and I'll give you a refund—no questions asked.

   Purchase your copy here. The sale ends tomorrow night at midnight.

   If you have any issues or questions, just hit me up in a reply. 😊

   —Andy

He's made a strong case already for his method, his ability to understand the root problems at play, and his expertise and authority. Now he simply sums up the offer:

- It's more than email content ("it's a visual treat").
- It's comprehensive (you won't be stuck searching the internet for hours trying to piece things together).
- It's tested ("detailed client result explanations . . . leave you feeling reassured and less alone").
- It's fast (no need to mess around with conflicting information; no need to ever backtrack—your time is valuable).
- It's safe (if you think that this doesn't match the quality of the content I've been sending you, you'll get an instant refund).

Email #6 (Friday AM)

Today is the last day to get *The Diet Adjustments Manual* at a 50 percent discount. 📖

I've received some great questions about the book. Here are the most common ones:

Who is this book for?
If you have come to the point where you understand the value in counting macros, but you have had unsuccessful fat loss and muscle growth phases in the past and wish to break your cycle of frustration, this is for you.

Who is this book NOT for?
If you are not prepared to pay attention to your calories and macros, this is not for you.

What is the difference between this and your other books on nutrition?
The RippedBody Nutrition Setup Guide and The Muscle and Strength Pyramid: Nutrition cover diet setup. This is a book about diet adjustments needed to keep you progressing once you have already done that.

Will you be making this available as a physical copy?
No. I'm keeping it digital so that I can continue to revise and build on it as I learn and develop as a coach. This also allows me to fulfill the "free updates forever" promise.

What do you mean by "free updates forever"?
Every time I update it, I will send you the new edition for free. I did this for all 3,600 previous buyers on March 24th.

I'm struggling with low-calorie intake, and I'm not sure how to adjust my macros to break the plateau. Will this help?

There are no tricks to get around the fact that calorie balance determines whether we gain, maintain, or lose weight. However, it is excruciatingly common to see people who think they have run into fat loss issues when they haven't; there is just some water retention masking it (or various other factors). The book is, essentially, dedicated to this issue. You will learn how to track your progress, assess whether you need to make a change, and know how to make changes if they are needed.

Does this book cover advice for older trainees?

There are some training considerations for older trainees, but I have seen absolutely no difference in how this book's nutrition adjustment principles play out with age. None. Yes, technically, metabolism does slow a little with age, but this pales in comparison to the slowing (adaptations) that happen when we diet, which the book teaches you how to navigate.

Is this book useful for women?

The client examples are all men because that is the population I coach, but the principles are just as relevant for women.

Which client results do you cover?

I have 54 pages of client data showing the principles of the book in action. These were the four most requested of my client results.

> ***Does this book cover training?***
> No, training is outside the scope of this book. But rest assured, there is nothing different from what you can read in the training articles on my site.
>
> ***Can I get a refund if it doesn't work?***
> Yes, there is a full, money-back guarantee. But if you apply the system, it will work. The only question is whether you're prepared to do it.
>
> **THE CHOICE IS YOURS . . .**
> You can follow in the footsteps of 4,300 others like you, or you can keep doing what you're doing.
> I have 10 years of experience coaching people. I'd love to show you exactly what to watch out for and how to do it right.
> Take advantage of that!
> » Get your lifetime copy now.
> If you have any questions, just hit reply. 🙏
> —Andy

This penultimate email is all about the offer—the thing Ripped-Body is selling. Who's it for? Who isn't it for? How does this compare to other books? All the usual things, none of which have much to do with trusting Andy and his team's ability to teach.

And then, a few hours later, right before the personal promotion window expires, the final "last call" email is sent out.

Email #7 (Friday PM)

> I always get a few people writing in saying they missed the deadline. I don't want this to be you.
>
> So, if you're always checking on your phone and been thinking you'll come back to this later, now's your last chance. The discount for *The Diet Adjustment Manual* expires in just a few hours (at midnight Eastern US time).
>
> *"It is one of those books that once you start reading it you can't let it go until you finish. What I like most is that it is coherent from start to end and I have all the details so that I can try to make the best decision for myself."* —Stefan Costache
>
> » Get lifetime access for 50 percent off now

There's not much that's truly unique about this pitch sequence. The model has been used countless times before (and we'll get more into it in the next chapter). But that's the beauty of it—it works.

Had the team sent this pitch just randomly out to subscribers, each with varying levels of awareness and understanding around nutrition as it relates to fitness, it wouldn't do nearly as well. Much of the sales pitch would need to be focused on the *need* for buying this book, rather than the *details* of the offer. But because of what Andy and his team have done, first by educating new subscribers with a highly engaging and personalized Lessons Sequence, and then by preparing for the promotion with the Bridge, they've ended up with a highly effective automated sales sequence that, without fail, begins every Monday and ends every Friday with new batches of subscribers.

The predictability of it is what's key. They know with high certainty what percentage of people who enter their L.B.P.S. will buy during their pitch. And every week, they're able (should they choose) to tweak different things about the promotion—for example, they can change the discount to something else, or swap out their FAQ list, and so on. This is what not only gives predictable and expected revenue each week, but it also allows them to come up with a value per subscriber. Get one new subscriber, and they're worth $X within two to three weeks of joining the L.B.P.S.

This is powerful. Once you have a value per L.B.P.S. subscriber, you can then quantify the return on investment for various acquisition campaigns. Things like:

- Running display ads to a cold audience that link to your L.B.P.S.
- Re-marketing to non-subscribers and non-customers who have visited your website with display ads for your L.B.P.S.
- Giving a talk at a conference and displaying a QR code at the end of the presentation that points to your L.B.P.S.
- Appearing on a podcast, and telling the listeners that if they want to dive deeper into what you were only able to gloss over during the last thirty minutes, they can go to YourLBPS.com (this is known as a vanity domain, which is something easy to say out loud and remember that simply redirects to the landing page to join your L.B.P.S.).
- Writing a guest post on another website and in the author byline (or, even better, mixed naturally into the post itself) link to your L.B.P.S.
- Encouraging subscribers to share your L.B.P.S. with their network, and rewarding them with discounts or other bonuses.

Now your entire marketing effort revolves around selling your L.B.P.S. to a wider audience. The L.B.P.S. handles learning about the individual *why* and *who* of each new person who joins, delivers a highly valuable educational sequence that's designed to prime them to be your perfect customer, and then bridges them to a promotion for an associated paid product or service.

You just need to sell the L.B.P.S. And the L.B.P.S. sells your brand and your products—entirely on autopilot.

Which brings us back to the subscriber valuation point I made previously. When you know the value per subscriber who enters your L.B.P.S., you can determine if your ad campaigns are paying off. If you're spending $1,000 to acquire two hundred new subscribers who, on average, generate $10 directly from your L.B.P.S., you've just created a machine that lets you put in $1,000 and spits out $2,000 within a few weeks. This is a machine you should figure out how to scale up *as significantly as possible*. It's exactly the sort of moneymaking machine you need for your business, and since some of those two hundred subscribers will likely hold off from buying for a few months or might end up telling a few of their friends about you, that initial $2,000 recouped investment yields many multiples over time.

Assuming that $10 per subscriber holds, why wouldn't you spend an hour on someone's podcast, deliver a big-picture overview of what you teach in your L.B.P.S., and then ask listeners to go deeper by joining your L.B.P.S.? If that episode ends up getting you five hundred new subscribers, you *know* you just made $5,000 for an hour appearance. And beyond just the money, you have five hundred people who now know about your brand, and five hundred people who are being delivered tremendously valuable information from you and your team.

I truly believe that creating an L.B.P.S. for your business will be your single most valuable email marketing project. If you only take one thing away from this book, it should be this.

Survey

Now we're at the final stage of the L.B.P.S.—the survey.

The majority of people who move through your L.B.P.S. won't end up buying during your pitch. That's totally normal and to be expected. However, there's only so much you as a marketer or business owner can do with a statistic like "6 percent bought during the pitch [which means 94 percent didn't buy]." How do you optimize that? How do you learn from that? Unless you're doing a lot of interviews with people who have recently completed your L.B.P.S., you're in the dark.

The survey is exactly what it sounds like: a simple questionnaire that asks someone to share what held them back from buying.

There are typically four reasons why someone would pass on your pitch (assuming, of course, you have a strong offer that solves a real problem):

- **Value:** "I don't think this is worth what you're charging."
- **Priority/Time:** "I have other things vying for my attention, and I need to focus on those first."
- **Trust:** "I want to solve this problem, but I'm not sure you can help."

And with a time-limited offer, I'd also add:

- **Missed:** "I was on a vacation the week you offered this. Oops."

If you could capture why someone declined or missed your promotion, you can use this on an aggregate level to uncover any big issues with your L.B.P.S.—maybe you're not really making a case for how crucial it is to solve this problem (priority) or anchoring what you're charging against what it's worth (value) or laying the groundwork to build a solid foundation of authority (trust). This data, taken as aggregate percentages, can and should be used to continually refine what you're saying and what you're offering.

But this feedback can also be used on an individual level to further segment your subscribers. By learning about why someone declined your offer and then attaching it to their contact record in your email platform, you can then use this the next time you decide to pitch them again on this offer—even if that's immediately or within the next few days.

I want to share an example of a training company that uses this one, single survey email to increase their overall L.B.P.S. performance. Spreadsheeto helps people with Microsoft Excel. They provide a number of products and training opportunities that are designed to not only learn more about how to use Excel, but to also justify getting a raise or a promotion in their workplace.

They run a pretty standard L.B.P.S., and the Monday following the ending of their personal promotion window, they send the following email:

> Hi there!
> First of all, thank you for reading our emails :)
> There goes a ton of work into everything we do, so when you support us by reading these emails, it means the world to us.

> According to our system, you didn't take advantage of the sale on *Zero to Hero*?
>
> That's fine, but . . .
>
> I would like to know why you didn't buy *Zero to Hero*. **Please click the link below that best represents your decision:**
>
> 1. "I'm interested, **but I missed the deadline**"
> 2. "**I don't have the time** to do the work"
> 3. "**It's too expensive**"
> 4. "**I don't know if you can help me** learn Excel"
> 5. "**I don't want to advance my career**"
>
> Knowing why gets us to know you better and helps us fine-tune our products.
>
> Thank you!
>
> Best regards
>
> Kasper Langmann
>
> Co-founder, Spreadsheeto

Each of the numbered-list options above are links that, when clicked, segment the subscriber based on their primary objection. The first four options track with the core objections or excuses that I listed above: value, priority, trust, or missing the deadline. Depending on what someone clicks, they're then either pitched immediately again with a limited twenty-four-hour promotion window (for example, if they missed last week's promotion entirely due to being on vacation), *or* they're queued up for a small educational sequence that dials in on their objection, and then offers a twenty-four-hour promotion window.

For example, if someone said that they don't have the time to do the work, what they're really saying is *it's not a priority for me right now*. We all have time, and few of us *truly* are overstretched, but for most people who select that option they're basically signaling that they're not quite sure that by going through the course and getting better at Excel that they're going to be able to get that pay raise or that cushy new promotion. To me, this means that Spreadsheeto failed to really drive home how important it is to drop what they're doing, boost their Excel skills, prove their new value to their employer, and then upgrade their lifestyle.

If someone does signal that Spreadsheeto's training isn't a priority for them, they're put into a small follow-up sequence that aims to fix that alignment "bug." They're given more examples of how people like themselves have transformed their career. They're reminded of the importance of making time for things that matter, and how the sooner they become more valuable to their employer, the sooner they can justify a pay raise. Then they're re-offered the same product at the same discount for twenty-four hours.

Mikkel Sciegienny, the founder of Spreadsheeto, was happy to share with me what results they've gotten from this email (these are averages across multiple weekly subscriber cohorts):

- **Twenty-two percent missed the deadline.** And **18.5 percent** of that group ended up purchasing when re-offered.
- **Twenty-one percent said they don't have the time.** Mikkel: "First, we explain to them how much time they'll save in the long run by investing a bit of time today on learning Excel. Then we dissect our course and show them exactly

how long it takes to go through the training. We also highlight our USPs like getting lifetime access and that the course is 100 percent self-paced." Of those, **4.5 percent** end up buying during the re-offer.

- **Forty-eight percent think it's too expensive.** Mikkel: "Here we try to reframe our course from an expense into an investment. We show and tell the subscriber that learning Excel can lead to a new/better job as well as a pay raise. We then send them an email, where we highlight our students' results after going through the training." **Six percent** buy during the re-offer.
- **Six percent don't trust Spreadsheeto.** They follow up by offering their money-back guarantee, send plenty of additional social proof, and show what's inside the training. **Two percent** buy during the re-offer.
- **Three percent select they don't want to get better at Excel.** Virtually no one who answers this goes on to buy.

Cumulatively, 8 percent of those who answer the survey end up deciding to ultimately buy. This has not only sizably improved the average value of an L.B.P.S. subscriber, but it's also given Spreadsheeto a big-picture understanding of their pitch. With almost half of those surveyed saying that the training is too expensive, this either means that the product genuinely *is* too pricey or, more likely, they're not doing a good enough job with positioning the offer as an investment. "Buy this, make more money."

By all accounts, this is a home run for Spreadsheeto. It's also a great example of pitch stacking, which is something we'll explore in the next chapter.

After the L.B.P.S.

Once you've delivered your survey and any follow-up pitches based on objections, you now need to set expectations with your subscriber about what's next. They've been getting some great information from you, have now been pitched on a complementary product or service, and it's time to let them know what they can expect going forward.

Here's where introducing a few of the concepts outlined in the Immersion Sequence example would make a lot of sense. While they're already probably quite familiar with your brand at this point, don't dismiss the importance of sending a few emails that highlight other resources of yours and make it clear how you communicate with your audience (you can find all this in the *Here's What's Next* email overview in the Immersion Sequence I covered earlier).

Chapter 7

PITCHING

This chapter is all about the art of the pitch. We're going to cover everything from the psychological triggers and holdbacks that people have when faced with a buying decision, along with more tactical concerns like what sort of urgency you should employ, whether to offer a single product, multiple, or tiers, and more.

WHAT ARE YOU ACTUALLY OFFERING?

A mistake I see a lot of marketers make when crafting a pitch sequence is to focus too much on the particulars: How long will the promotion run? How many emails are going to be sent? Should we include any sort of visual countdown timer? And so on.

While these questions are important, it's best to start with the fundamentals. Who are you pitching to, why should they care, and what are you asking of them? Specifically, you want to ask yourself the following questions:

1. **Who's getting this?** Are you sending it to everyone? Or just to existing customers? Or some other segment? This is your target audience, and unless you're doing a big seasonal promotion it rarely makes sense to pitch your entire list. (If someone just joined your list a few hours ago, it might leave a bad impression if the first emails they start getting from you are heavy-hitting sales emails.)

2. **What level of product or problem-awareness does your target audience have?** If it's a new product, have you been building anticipation over email for it? Is your target audience eager for it? The importance of this point changes depending on the offer you present. For example, a deeply discounted suite of products sold over Black Friday will likely end up getting plenty of people who have no idea whether they actually truly need what you're offering, but who just like a good deal. Typically, the more expensive the product or service, the more this point matters.

3. **What has someone been receiving from you recently?** Did you just recently promote something to your audience? There's a good chance they might be a bit burned out, and you should instead be sending more trust- and authority-building emails for a while. Or maybe you have been sending out regularly educational emails—is your audience prepared for what you're about to pitch to them?

4. **What's special about your offer?** If you're pitching something that's already available on your website, why should they buy now? What, if any, urgency accompanies your offer? (We'll get more into this shortly.)

5. **Why now?** Why should your target audience drop what they're doing and act now?

6. **What's the next step?** Is it to click over to a long sales page? Are you linking directly to a payment form? Are you asking for a reply? How are your emails preparing them to take this next step?

SHOULD YOU USE URGENCY?

When pitching a product or service, there's a good chance that it's going to be available for purchase outside of your promotion window. You know this, and your subscribers likely know this. While it's true that there are some businesses that *only* allow you to buy certain products when they're being actively promoted within an email pitch, they're the exception rather than the norm.

You want your pitch emails to generate sales. And for this to happen, you're going to need to do more than say, "You can buy this thing . . . that's been available over here for a while . . . and will continue to be available."

For many of us, our natural state is busyness. When you're pitching via email, I might tell myself I'm interested, but you're contacting me at the wrong time. So, while I'm not going to buy, I will buy *later*. At least this is what we tell ourselves. But most people won't come back. Remember: no one is as interested in your product or service as you and your team are.

I strongly recommend that anytime you're pitching over email that you include urgency. "Here's what we're offering, here's why it's better than the usual deal, and here's how long you have to get it." After all, if you're delivering something truly great, you want your subscribers to put away any excuses they have in taking that next step. The sooner you're able to help them, the better off they'll be.

TEN METHODS OF CREATING URGENCY

When you're intent on getting someone to take action during your pitch, there are a number of methods that you can use to create urgency. Ultimately, all that really matters is that whatever you're using to incentivize those on the receiving end is worth them acting *today*.

The most common, and inarguably often the most effective, urgency method is to provide a **discount**. If you want to see this in action, just look at the annual circus that is Black Friday / Cyber Monday. Here you provide a discount, either expressed as a fixed amount or a percentage. People love getting great deals, so don't "discount" discounting.

One downside to discounting is that it can end up conditioning your subscribers to always expect a discount. Discounting can also cheapen your brand—there's a reason high-end luxury goods are really never on "sale." We've all seen retail shops that always have a sale going on, and we know that no one is ever dumb enough to pay sticker price. If that's the sort of business you want and it makes sense for you financially, then that's totally fine.

Other methods of discounting include:

— **Bundling:** Offer additional products for free, either as standard during your pitch, or if they hit a specific threshold of spending.

- **Limited Time:** It might make sense to *only* have your product be available to purchase during a limited-time pitch window. You often see this with more premium online courses that open for enrollment every few months. Outside of those enrollment windows, there's no way to join.
- **Extended Trial:** If you're selling software, a membership site, or anything that might have a trial period, either offer a free or greatly reduced trial, or extend the trial you already offer. The software company Ahrefs regularly incentivizes by selling a seven-day free trial of their analytics software for $1.
- **Concierge Setup:** If you're something that might be tricky to get up and running, you could offer a concierge setup program where someone from your team will work one-on-one with your new customers to get them using your product, provide strategic advice on how to use it, and answer any questions they might have in the process.
- **Strategy Call:** Service providers often provide high-value consultations totally free of charge. The downside, however, is no-show rates are exceptionally high. The potential client just doesn't have any skin in the game. If you can instead offer a fixed price initial consult or strategy call, publicly advertise what you charge for it, and then offer it for free for anyone who decides to book during your pitch window, you're then able to reposition the free call as something valuable.
- **Higher Tiers:** Offer a free upgrade to a higher tier or plan if they purchase within your pitch window. "Get the Gold plan for the price of the Silver plan."

- **Free or Expedited Shipping:** Buy during the pitch window and we'll cover your priority shipping costs.
- **Quarterly Reviews:** This is specific to B2B providers, especially those who sell software. You could offer expert-level reviews by your team once a quarter of their account: what's going well, what needs improvement, and so on. This also does wonders for reducing cancellations.
- **Good Ol' Swag:** Offer free gear like shirts, mugs, hats, or whatever else. You'd need to have a very fashionable and desirable brand to pull this off.

The methods I listed above all impact your profit per sale, but the goal is to add *more* customers than you would have otherwise by getting them to take action now rather than having them register in the back of their head: "This sounds great . . . but I'm busy. I'll revisit this later . . ." (And we all know most won't!)

HOW LONG SHOULD YOUR PITCH RUN FOR?

When setting up a new time-sensitive pitch, you're going to need to answer how time-sensitive your promotion window actually is. While there's no exact science to this, there are a few best practices that should serve as a good starting point. Like with anything, pitch duration (along with your urgency method, etc.) should be something you continuously test.

The longer the promotion window, the more emails you'll want to send. Each email's job is going to be to qualify your target audience: Is this ultimately right for you, or wrong for you?

Here are some of the factors that should go into figuring out your pitch window.

How Expensive Is What I'm Offering?

Price, and how appealing your offer ultimately is, is probably going to be the most important factor in determining the duration of your promotion window.

A product offered at $100 primarily to an email list of students is going to perform much differently than another $100 product sold to successful business owners. So you want to ensure that you have a strong understanding of *who* your audience is so you can determine how price sensitive they are to your offer, and what sort of budget decisions (if any) they'll need to make before acting on your offer.

One rule of thumb I use, primarily when selling to businesses (or at least individuals wearing the "business owner" hat—e.g., freelancers), is the following:

- < $100 offer, 2–3 days
- $100–$500 offer, 3–5 days
- $500+ offer, 5–9 days

Ultimately, though, this is all going to come down to how prepared someone is for your offer. Do they already know they need it? Do they know the product or service you're offering exists, or are they being blindsided by something new? How incredible is the offer, based both on the product itself and whatever discount or bonus is accompanying it?

How Prepared Is My Target Audience?

Imagine this: You join the email list of a personal finance blog. The very next day, because the company is pitching their entire list—which includes people who have been on their list for years, along with you—you're pitched on a rather pricey online course on how to trade options in the stock market. You're not really sure what options are or what they have to do with the stock market. You're by no means ready for this product.

This offer is probably going to fall flat for you. You're not ready for it. At all. This is a common mistake marketers make when using the "spray and pray" method of pitching their audience. They target their entire audience, which includes people who are new to the list, veterans to it, highly engaged, and those who are mostly tuned out. While these pitches end up working—after all, this pattern continues again and again—it tends to heavily alienate those who aren't ready for the offer, and that alienation often leads to high unsubscribe rates.

I'm a big proponent of the L.B.P.S. model that I covered in the last chapter. This ensures that people are familiar with the problem at hand, learn how it can be solved, and then are presented with a strong offer that helps them solve it. There's no reason you can't create a similar L.B.P.S.-style sequence outside of onboarding and welcoming new subscribers. The most common way of doing this is to have a few weeks of educational emails go out in advance of the pitch that focus on the problem your offer helps solve. This way, when you do open up your promotion window, at least your target audience is familiar with the problem space your offer exists in (and you should ideally exclude new people who didn't get those educational emails from receiving your pitch).

How Much "Friction" Is Involved?

My first software company was online project management software, and I was naive enough to think that the biggest roadblock to adoption was the price. I obsessed over what I'd charge monthly, and how I'd set up and price each plan that I offered.

It wasn't until I started talking to people, especially those who tried the software but didn't buy it, that I realized there was so much more at play than just cost. I heard that people loved the product, but they couldn't get their team to actually use it. Or they came across the product, liked what they saw, but didn't have an actual project to use it on. I also was told that they just couldn't get their clients using it, and without client interaction they couldn't experience most of the benefits of Planscope.

These were all roadblocks that had zero to do with the price. Without a project, without their team, and without their clients using the product, it wasn't actually that useful. Other software products, like Baremetrics, simply require you to sign up, integrate it with your payment gateway with a few clicks, and a few minutes later all of your historical sales and customer data comes to life on your brand-new dashboard. Baremetrics has little friction in between liking what you read on the website and getting value from the product.

The more friction between intrigue and getting use out of your product, the more emails you'll want to send that coach people through how to get to that end goal. With Planscope, that meant sending dedicated emails that covered how to get your team involved, how to start with just a simple test project (even if you don't have a new client to try it with yet), and how Planscope makes it super easy for clients. These emails covered the various features, like email notifications and weekly reports, that could preemptively counter the objection of: "Ugh, more software I need to learn how to use."

How Many Stakeholders Are Involved

Not everyone on your email list has unilateral purchasing authority. Spouses, department heads, bosses, and others often need to sign off in order for a purchase to happen, and if you're just speaking to one of the parties involved then there's a good chance you're not going to sell as easily as you might like.

SmashingConf is a conference hosted multiple times a year by the team at *Smashing Magazine*. Their audience is creatives who work on the web, and the majority of the people on their email list are employees of companies that hire creatives. When promoting their events, they send their subscribers a "Convince the Boss" PDF that they can easily forward over to their boss. Because, sure, what employee wouldn't want a paid vacation to San Francisco for a few days! But the boss, the person paying the bills and losing a few days of productivity for that employee, might not be as excited about SmashingConf.

I love the "Convince the Boss" letter that SmashingConf sends to their subscribers:[13]

6 REASONS WHY YOU SHOULD SEND YOUR INCREDIBLY HARD-WORKING, DESERVING EMPLOYEE TO SMASHINGCONF

1. STAY AHEAD OF THE CURVE
   When it comes to digital experiences, we often compare it to swimming upstream. If you stop swimming, you don't stand still, instead you get swept backward. Our digital channels will become dated, and customers will stop using them. Worse still, our competition will get further ahead until catching up becomes impossible.

2. ESSENTIAL SKILLS
   We know your designer and developers are an essential component of your team. That's why it's vital to invest in their skills. Digital experiences are a critical component of all businesses. The jobs of so many people are changing because of digital. In the fast-paced web industry it's never been more important to be up to date with the latest technologies, trends, and design processes—and at SmashingConf, that's what we deliver!

3. IDEAL LOCATION
   Our conference and workshop venue, the Fort Mason Center, is located on Marina Boulevard at Buchanan Street, along the northern waterfront. (It has world-class bay views, too!)

4. RELIVE THE CONFERENCE
    Throughout the conference, we gather all the information in a handy Google Document so that attendees can share their learnings with other team members or managers afterward. What's more, we provide attendees with online videos and slides of all sessions!

5. PRACTICAL TAKEAWAYS
    Learn how others failed, so that you won't have to make the same mistakes. You will also discover techniques, strategies, and tooling to get to better results, faster.

6. NETWORKING OPPORTUNITIES
    Plenty of structured and informal networking sessions mean tons of opportunities to forge new contacts and talk with like-minded designers and developers. Our speakers are always willing to chat outside sessions, and our workshops provide a focused opportunity to get feedback from the experts on all sorts of design questions.

Notice how brilliant so many of these points are, especially when perceived by the boss of the employee who's asking to go to SmashingConf:

- Your employees are becoming less valuable over time if they're not constantly learning new things. We help fix that.
- We know not everyone from your team will be able to attend, but the attending employees will bring back a Google Document that has everything that was covered. You'll also get the videos that can then be shared around the office.

- Your employees will learn stuff that helps them do their work better and faster.
- They might meet some interesting people who would love to work with your team. Think of this as a recruitment opportunity.

The decision maker now isn't thinking, "The flights will cost . . . The hotel . . . The conference ticket . . . And we're going to need to put a halt on things for a few days . . ." Now they're being shown how they'll get back an even more valuable team member, who can share his or her learnings with the team.

"FAST MOVER BONUSES"

Longer promotion windows tend to get a number of up-front sales when an offer is launched, then sales plummet for a few days, and then on the final day lots of sales come through just hours and minutes before the promotion expires.

To help normalize sales, some brands use "fast mover bonuses" that provide a super impressive initial offer, followed by a not-so-super but still impressive offer. Growth Tools provides business coaching to hundreds of companies. When they pitch their coaching over email, they'll often introduce their service offering by promoting a free strategy call as a bonus.

This effectively allows something like the following to take place:

- **Days 1–3:** Initial offer promoting limited-time enrollment into their coaching program, along with a free initial strategy call with the team.
- **Days 4–7:** Promotion of limited-time enrollment into their coaching program.

This allows for an initial burst of sales on the first day, another burst on the third, and another burst on the seventh. The first few days are designed to really push the free strategy call, whereas the remainder of the promotion window is focused on the value of their coaching platform.

Here's how Growth Tools announces that their fast mover bonus is expiring:

> Quick reminder here to schedule your free strategy call with our team as this bonus expires today.
>
> On this call we'll do three things:
>
> - Deep Dive: Learn more about your business so we can understand how it works and can coach and advise you well.
> - Blind Spot Analysis: We'll walk you through the common blind spots and help you start to identify your biggest area of opportunity.
> - If it seems like it would be a good fit, we'll show you what it would look like for us to work together 1:1.
>
> We've done this with hundreds of businesses with those clients seeing an average revenue increase of 35 percent in the first 3 months.
>
> This is a free bonus that expires today, so be sure to take advantage!

WHY DIDN'T YOU BUY?

You'll recall that when describing the L.B.P.S. system for onboarding new subscribers and pitching them on a relevant product or service, the "S" stood for surveying. *"What held you back from buying?"*

This is something that should be added to almost all of your pitches. It's a great way to uncover insights into why people don't buy, and these insights can be used to help refine future promotions. This data can also be attached to individual subscribers, so that the next time you pitch somebody on the same product or service you could send them more relevant content that homes in on the specific purchasing objection they previously had.

There are typically four reasons why someone would pass on your pitch:

- **Value:** "I don't think this is worth what you're charging."
- **Priority/Time:** "I have other things vying for my attention, and I need to focus on those first."
- **Trust:** "I want to solve this problem, but I'm not sure you can help."

And with a time-limited offer, I'd also add:

- **Missed:** "I was on a vacation the week you offered this. Oops."

(If this seems familiar, I listed these out when describing the L.B.P.S. system earlier.)

What you want is to send an email or a series of emails a few days after your promotion window expires. There are a few models for what you should ask in these emails and how to write them, so I'll cover each and then provide my recommendation.

The first way to do this is to ask for an open-ended reply. It can be as simple as:

> Hi there,
>
> Last week, we promoted <name of product or service>, and it looks like you didn't end up buying.
>
> To help us improve, would you mind taking a minute to reply to this email and let us know:
>
> If you CONSIDERED purchasing, what held you back from buying?
>
> If you DIDN'T consider purchasing, what would you have expected to see offered instead?
>
> Hit "Reply" and let us know. Our team reads and replies to every email.

While this is perfectly fine, it is asking quite a bit from people. Why should they bother taking the time to reply? They're also going to need to think back and try to remember specifically what they were thinking a few days ago (that's assuming they actually saw, read, and considered what you sent them!).

From my own experience and other email marketers I've spoken to, the above approach also tends to attract the "extremes." These are the people who *really* wanted to like you and your offer, but there was something big—something often philosophical—that stood in the way. For example, you might include access to a customer-only Facebook group with purchase. And instead of getting substantive answers that you can actually work with, you'll end up with a few very loud, and frankly very fringe, opinions of people who believe Meta and Mark Zuckerberg are members of the Illuminati and felt it necessary to send your team a novella detailing how you're propping up the Evil Empire by using Facebook for your customer community.

I prefer a "click the best option" approach, like the one Spreadsheeto uses:

> Hi there!
>
> First of all, thank you for reading our emails :)
>
> There goes a ton of work into everything we do, so when you support us by reading these emails, it means the world to us.
>
> According to our system, you didn't take advantage of the sale on *Zero to Hero*.
>
> That's fine, but . . .
>
> I would like to know why you didn't buy *Zero to Hero*? **Please click the link below that best represents your decision:**
>
> 1. "I'm interested, **but I missed the deadline**"
> 2. "**I don't have the time** to do the work"
> 3. "**It's too expensive**"
> 4. "**I don't know if you can help me** learn Excel"
> 5. "I **don't want to advance my career**"
>
> Knowing why gets us to know you better and helps us fine-tune our products.
>
> Thank you!
>
> Best regards
>
> Kasper Langmann
>
> Co-founder, Spreadsheeto

Here you're not asking someone to go and reply—you're simply asking them to click a link. The other upside to this method is that each link can be set up to segment the subscriber who clicked it, so when someone selects "it's too expensive" that data can be stored on their subscriber record, allowing you to send specialized campaigns in the future that directly address and focus on the issue of cost.

The downside? There's only so much you can do with statistics like: "32 percent say they don't have the time." This is why a hybrid approach is best. Someone clicks on "don't have the time," and they're brought to a web form that says something like, "Would you mind sharing with us why you don't have the time (e.g., family, work, or other commitments)?"

An approach like this gives you plenty of quantitative data that you can easily chart and use for email segmentation, and it also gives you raw, voice-of-customer qualitative data that color specific objections with the response to a pointed question that relates exactly to their primary purchasing objection.

PITCH STACKING

It's easy to think of promotions as a one-and-done thing. You pitch a product or service, and then you go back to educational emails for a while. Later on, you come back and pitch the same thing. And the cycle repeats ad infinitum.

While this definitely works and is how most of us who sell over email do things, you can also think about finding ways to stack the same offer using multiple pitching mediums. I once put together an L.B.P.S. system for a financial services company that primarily pitched their offer—a complimentary strategy consultation—over email. While the system worked really well, there were a lot of people who wanted to just be able to ask questions to someone in a live format. What we ended up doing was setting them up with a monthly live training webinar that really rehashed much of what was taught within the L.B.P.S. The difference: there was an actual person delivering the training. You could see them. You could hear them. And at the end, you could use your microphone to ask them questions and they'd respond directly to you.

Every week, another cohort of new subscribers would move through the funnel. Some booked the strategy consultation; most didn't. Their email marketing system was then set up to grab everyone who didn't and promote their monthly live webinar, which included a few dates and time options, to non-buyers. From doing just this, they were able to nearly double the effectiveness of their L.B.P.S. and give their accounts team a limitless stream of new leads.

COMING UP WITH VALUATIONS

Data-driven marketers don't work off gut assumptions; they look at the data. And the brilliant thing about something as scalable as email marketing is that you're able to collect a lot of data, and run many tests and experiments, quickly.

You're going to want to determine a few initial key metrics that you'll revise from time to time. These metrics will give you the confidence to know what's working and what isn't, and the data you need to experiment correctly.

Value per Customer (Lifetime)

This is simply your total revenue divided by your total number of customers. Your brand has brought in ten million dollars, and you have one hundred thousand customers. This puts the average value of a customer at an even $100.

Unfortunately, this metric loses accuracy, especially as your business ages. Consider a customer who bought something five years ago and hasn't bought anything since. They'd still be included in this valuation, even though they haven't actually bought from you in quite some time. And any attempts to optimize this number will be really slow moving, since you're always going to be struggling against the weight of historical transaction data.

Value per Customer (Annually)

This number ends up being much more useful. Here you're taking the revenue generated this year and dividing it by the number of unique customers who bought this year, both new customers and returning.

You can then run these calculations against their previous period. If this book helps you get serious about email marketing and you decide to really focus on doing it right, you can then take a year's worth of data after you've set up your new email system and compare it to the previous year.

Value per Customer (By Channel)

You're going to want to track the initial acquisition channel for each subscriber in your database. These channels might include:

- Specific ad campaigns
- Live events where you've captured new leads
- Podcast interviews

- Search engines, and the type of content or article someone saw that led them to opt in
- Guest or sponsored posts
- Link exchanges
- Social media
- Referrals from your subscribers

By applying the same calculation as I listed above, but by splitting the results by key acquisition channels, you can see exactly what financial impact each channel has on your bottom line. This is especially important for the pay-to-play channels, like display ads or booths at a conference.

Value per Customer (By Segment)

The *who* and *why* data, along with any other segmentation data that you capture through surveying, can also be leveraged to uncover how different types of buyers are valued relative to each other.

This is used to either:

1. **Determine who your "MVP" customers are.** What industry do they work in? What's their job role? What primary need led them to join your list?
2. **Uncover the inverse.** What types of customers just aren't spending much with you?

MVP segments should have marketing spend prioritized to find more people like that. If a certain industry is spending gobs of money with you, find more people in that industry. Sponsor their events. Find out who's focused on supporting that group and partner with them.

The lagging segments probably shouldn't be written off. In some cases, you *might* just accept that certain segments just aren't great customers. A company that provided recruiting management solutions I helped a few years back learned that one of the segments they tracked was just a horrible customer. That segment? College students (specifically ones who were doing research into recruiting best practices).

But in most cases, the problem probably has to do with you. Are you losing them somehow? Maybe they're not being sent case studies from people like them who have used your product or service. Or you're leveraging language that just doesn't resonate with them. I like to look at an unexpectedly low segment valuation as a fantastic "bug report" that shows that the marketing material we've created is largely falling on deaf ears.

Value per Subscriber (Lifetime)

Now we'll turn our attention to subscriber valuation, which gives you an indication of the total value of your email list—both customers and non-customers alike. The idea here is that if you've generated ten million dollars in revenue and you have one hundred thousand customers and one million subscribers, your value per subscriber is $10.

And like with your lifetime value per customer, this doesn't really help all that much. To be truly representative, your subscriber count would need to be your *total* count, and not just the number of your *current* subscribers. (Most email platforms just show you your total active subscribers, which subtracts out anyone who's unsubscribed.)

Value per Subscriber (Annually)

This valuation is pretty straightforward: Begin with how many subscribers you started the year with, add the total number of new subscribers you gained, subtract the number that unsubscribed, and then divide the revenue attributed to email for the year by that figure.

Value per Subscriber (By Channel)

Same as the value per customer by channel, but now take all subscribers (and not just customers) who came from a particular channel.

Value per Subscriber (By Segment)

Same as the value per customer by channel, but now take all subscribers (and not just customers) and split up their overall valuations by the segment data you're tracking.

Value per Subscriber (Within a Month)

This value is especially useful if you're leaning heavily on using L.B.P.S. systems to onboard and pitch new subscribers on your products or services. Because these systems usually span just a few weeks in duration, if you can quantify the overall value of a subscriber within a month of joining your list you can give yourself a metric that can yield almost real-time feedback on the performance of both your acquisition campaigns and the onboarding and pitching systems that do the heavy lifting early on in the relationship with a new subscriber.

For example, let's say over the last month you've added one thousand new subscribers. Most of this traffic came from a mixture of paid ad campaigns and referrals, and almost all of these subscribers were funneled into your primary L.B.P.S. system. Of that group, fifteen ended up unsubscribing during that window and forty-eight purchased at an average cart value of $229.

By employing a bit of back-of-the-napkin math, that cohort of 985 generated $10,992 in revenue. (Note that we're subtracting out the churn, or unsubscribers, from the cohort's total.) This puts the value of each unique subscriber at $11.16, with your L.B.P.S. having a 4.9 percent average conversion rate.

Yes, that's a lot of math. But let's break down how useful this is for you.

First off, you're paying an ad provider like Google or Facebook an amount per click. Not everyone who clicks ends up joining your email list, so you're going to want to quantify how much money you've actually spent on ads during that window. If you spent above $10,992, you've lost money. Otherwise, you've discovered the Golden Goose: making ads profitable.

But even if you're losing money by paying more for ads than you're getting before the ad bill is due, this might not necessarily be a bad thing. If you knew that your value per subscriber annually was $30, you're looking at that cohort of new subscribers generating something close to $30,000 in the next twelve months. Only you, and I suppose your bank account, can figure out whether the calculus makes sense here. "Do we lose $2 per new subscriber initially, but end up netting a profit of $18 per subscriber by the end of the year?"

What matters is that you have this data on hand. It's something you can work with. You can experiment with it. You can tweak and toy with various levers in your email system to make improvements that have effects across your entire email system.

Let's look at how you can do this . . .

HOW TO READ YOUR VALUATION DATA

Once you've put a value on your customers and your subscribers, and have spliced and diced that figure down by acquisition channel and segment, it's now time to get strategic. You're probably going to be somewhat surprised what you uncover, and ask yourself questions like:

- Why does this segment of subscriber have such a low customer valuation? (Answer: it means they rarely turn into paying customers.)
- Why is this channel's customer value and subscriber value so similar? (Answer: they convert brilliantly.)
- Why is the value per subscriber annually not much higher than the value per subscriber within a month? (Answer: you're not doing nearly enough to extract more revenue from people outside of your L.B.P.S.)

Data allows you to make informed decisions. But most importantly, the decisions you decide to make can be easily verified. An L.B.P.S. that generates $11.16 can be tested to have a totally different set of lessons, promote a different offer, or shake up the urgency method used. Within a few weeks, you'll know if the new valuation is above or below your existing control. If it's higher, keep it and start thinking of your new test. Otherwise, backtrack and try again.

Chapter 8

PLAYING THE LONG GAME

The standard model for email marketing is to create a gentle interplay between promotion and nurturing. Some emails are designed to sell, while others are meant to build trust and authority. In the last chapter, we explored how to create the emails that make you money. But if all you're doing is pitching, you're going to exhaust your email list. They're going to grow weary of your constant attempt to take their money. While this approach can work in some specific circumstances (like Groupon, who sends daily emails announcing limited-time deals they've sourced), most brands need to do more than just outright sell.

We all have domain expertise that others don't. If you work at a financial services company, you know a lot more about investing than the average person. Accountants know a lot about the nuances of taxation. Web agencies know a lot about what goes into building a great website. Nike and Adidas know a lot about training.

Don't dismiss domain expertise as something your customers don't really care about. People trust experts, and trust leads to interaction. Buyers rarely like to go into something blind. While there's a degree of truth to the assumption that most of us *really* don't care about the intricacies of the IRS tax code, most of us would like to know what we should have our bookkeeper do, or what sort of tax rebates we should be keeping, and so on. We also want to feel like we have some idea of what's going on when talking to our accountant.

Don't be afraid to use your domain expertise to get new customers. In the ever-increasing land grab for consumer attention, one of the best ways of coming out on top is to be a partner and ally, not just be a vendor or seller of something. A well-thought-out, long-term nurturing strategy can do just that.

In this chapter, we'll look at how to create the glue that ties your pitch efforts together. What we cover will help you keep your list "warm" and will also serve to passively sell your products and services alongside the nurturing content you'll be sending. Best of all, eventually this, too, will be able to be automated. While I'm by no means a lazy marketer (actually . . . I am), I do find that the more time my team and I can spend outside of messing around in our email platform, the better. That's time that we can spend getting more subscribers, creating more products, and doing more meaningful stuff away from a computer.

SENDING ORIGINAL CONTENT

Long gone are the days of boring company newsletters that showcase participation at a charity golf event or the recent holiday party. The modern newsletter is, in a way, providing an alternative to the traditional form of online content marketing: blogging.

Blogs are typically optimized for search traffic, and many of the top-performing articles have a wealth of keyword research behind them that leads to creating the perfect blog post to please the Google machine. Email newsletters can be used to deliver educational content marketing, but to an audience you already have and who has given you permission to reach out to them.

Email newsletters are optimized for engagement, which is marketing speak for trying to get as many of your subscribers as possible to open your emails, read what you have to say, click on whatever you want them to click on, and with hope *not* click the "Unsubscribe" link in the footer. Because these educational emails aren't being optimized for a machine (Google), but are instead written for people, they can be largely conversational and eschew many of the rote structural requirements that generally accompany high-ranking blog posts.

Your email newsletters should be written to do some combination of the following:

- Establish your brand's expertise in the domain you operate in
- Create authority in the minds of your readers
- Detail the problems associated with your domain, which your products and services help solve
- Highlight the gravity of these problems not being solved
- Curate stories and examples of other people who both operate in this domain and have been affected by, and have overcome, domain problems
- Offer tactical advice and frameworks
- Provide motivational support

They should also be cadenced. If you write and send a weekly newsletter, you should make it clear to your audience that you send original content every week. The more your readers get used to seeing your brand in their inbox—*especially* when providing free and valuable content, rather than just pushing a sale—the better.

GoodRx, an American telemedicine provider, regularly sends content to their list that helps their readers understand the ins and outs of medical research. How do you choose the right blood pressure medication? Is there a cure for diabetes? They want their audience to associate GoodRx with being the brand that's responsible for broadening their medical knowledge. That way, when a reader questions, "Yes, but can MY diabetes be cured?" they turn to GoodRx. The company also stays on top of updates to medical legislation and enrollment periods for things like Medicare:

> **Medicare Annual Enrollment period is here.**
> We've partnered with GoHealth to help you start the Medicare enrollment screening process and guide you through the Annual Enrollment Period, from 10/15–12/7. GoHealth can assist you in finding the Medicare savings and benefits that meet your needs . . .
> Need more information to help you choose the right plan?
> Call a licensed GoHealth insurance agent at . . .

In the above example, GoodRx is using their brand's authority and influence to partner with GoHealth, who specializes in medical insurance.

HubSpot is another great example, and for some *the* example, of a brand that does email marketing right. They realize that they have a high-price offering and there's a lot of prep work that needs to go into acquiring a new customer. So they play the long game. They send emails about, well, email: what to send, how to write subject lines that improve open rates, what automation is, how to integrate your customer relationship management (CRM) software with your email database, and more.

It's easy to focus entirely on the impact of email marketing on *direct* sales, asking, "How much revenue did this email campaign generate for us?" But an often-overlooked side effect of pushing out tremendous amounts of valuable information to your audience is that it's likely to get shared.

HubSpot sends great content to their audience—ranging from those who barely know what HubSpot is, to customers who pay Hub-Spot tens of thousands of dollars a year. And the people who benefit from this content are apt to share the content on social media platforms or by simply forwarding a newsletter to a colleague. This creates a bit of a viral loop: create content, send it to your list, your list shares the content with their network, this adds more people to your list (because some end up filling out your email opt-in forms), and on and on the cycle goes.

Increasing Your Luck Surface Area

This hit home with me when I was starting to seriously scale up my agency in the mid-2000s. We weren't very savvy when it came to email marketing (few were back then!), but we did host a number of in-person networking events and seminars at our office. As the owner / person responsible for bringing in sales, my focus was always on the "whales" who showed up. Who actually owned a business and could pay our rates? Those were the people I cared about because I was myopically focused on turning attendees of our events into new clients.

But then we were approached in early 2011 by the marketing manager of one of the presidential candidates who was a favorite to win. His nephew had attended a few of our events and really liked what we stood for and what we had to say. I was excited as hell by the idea of adding a potential U.S. president to our client roster (despite the fact that half the team hated the guy). We ended up winning the contract, I got my portfolio entry, and it was all because the nephew (who was currently in college) of the aforementioned marketing manager learned a lot of interesting stuff from us at our free events.

Had I just admitted "whales" to our events, we would have missed this opportunity. And unless I was in a very charitable mood, I would have never met for coffee with a college student to talk business (but I absolutely would have for a Fortune 500 executive). It just wouldn't make sense to sacrifice so much one-on-one time to low- or no-value opportunities. But when I'm hosting an event or sending out an email campaign to thousands of people, it doesn't matter how many people are on the receiving end. If I present a seminar to a room of ten people or a room of fifty, the only real change for me is maybe how much time I need to dedicate to questions at the end. I still need to show up and present for an hour. The size of the audience is immaterial.

And that's really the magic of email. You can send valuable content to fifty, five hundred, or five hundred thousand people and the time and effort your team puts into creating and sending that email probably doesn't change. By doing this, you're able to expand your "luck surface area." Even if some of the people on your list don't seem like they'd ever become customers or clients of yours, don't discount their ability to become vocal brand advocates.

After the referral that led to working with a presidential candidate, I started to reason through what ultimately led to us getting the project. We had no direct connection to anyone on the campaign. We weren't privy to any requests for proposals they were sending out. What got us the job was a chance conversation that happened over Thanksgiving. Our team had materially benefited the student. He learned so much about *real* business because of us, and he put us on a pedestal in our local community. We were a team that gave in abundance, and if you're entrepreneurially minded at all and live in southeastern Virginia, you want to be a part of what this team's doing.

In his mind, we had made him better, and so he wanted to share this newfound improvement with anyone he thought might benefit. This is exactly what happens when past clients refer new work your way: you made them better off, so they're more likely to tell their peers about you. The equation is straightforward. Give away value, make better, create advocates. But there's only so many new clients or customers you can add, especially if you run a services company similar to my agency, where we could only handle so many clients at once. This impedes your ability to scale your referral network.

But what about when you're giving another form of value? Or when you're sending bulk emails? Or delivering talks in front of a lot of people at once? The sky's the limit in terms of how many vocal advocates you can create then. And these advocates are the ones who are going to tell others about you. While many will never actually become paying customers of yours, don't discount what sort of effect chance encounters with advocates of your brand and people who have never heard of you can have.

DIGEST EMAILS

Not every team has the ability to send new, long-form original content to their audience every week or even every month. Fortunately, you don't necessarily need to always be creating lengthy and original articles in order to deliver valuable content.

There's a growing number of newsletters that are digests of curated information—videos, podcast interviews, articles, or even Twitter threads. While the brand behind these emails doesn't take responsibility for having produced any of the shared content, the organization and curation of the content shared boosts the authority and credibility of the sender.

James Clear, author of *Atomic Habits*, has topped the *New York Times* bestseller list for a few years now. (At the time of writing this book, it's *still* dominating.) How it got there is largely thanks to sending out a weekly digest. The author's newsletter, available at JamesClear.com, goes out every Thursday. It's a curated list of three short ideas from James, two quotes from other people, and a question that's designed to get the reader engaging in self-reflection every week.

These emails all include subtle promotion for his book, and he regularly announces when retailers like Amazon are running sales on *Atomic Habits*. While there's undoubtedly plenty of behind-the-scenes referrals happening between readers of the book and featured placements in retail shops, the email list is really what made the book sell. By the time it launched, over four hundred thousand people a week were tuning in to get James's 3-2-1 newsletter. His weekly audience now numbers in the millions. This is every author's dream: the ability to connect individually with their readers, sans any third-party retailers like Amazon or Barnes & Noble.

James is mostly interested in book sales, and the money he makes per sale doesn't make sense to have him and the team that helps him manage his writing business solicit replies from readers. But for some businesses, especially those selling services that are five figures and up, curation can also be a great way to create sales conversations at scale.

I once worked with a law firm that built up a lot of authority over email, largely with an email list made up of local business owners. Every few weeks, they'd send out a short email that listed a few interesting articles they came across—largely in the digital patents and trademarks space. It's the sort of material that any lawyer involved in patents and trademarks knows all about. After all, staying abreast of updates in the industry they practice in is, quite literally, their job. But to us laymen who tangentially were interested in patents and trademarks because we were creating products that we wanted to secure, we wanted to know a bit, but not *that much*.

The emails the law firm sent would link to articles or discussions around key changes in legislation or case law, along with predictions about what was going to happen next. Below each link, they'd write a short paragraph that summed up their thoughts on the article and what their big takeaways were. These blurbs weren't full of industry jargon or whatever else. They were written explicitly by a lawyer who knows this world and translated to make total sense to normal businesspeople.

At the end of every email, they'd include a short and concise call to action: *"Do any of these new developments affect your business? Or do you have any questions or concerns about any of this new legislation? Tap reply and let us know. One of our lawyers will get back to you today with an answer."*

This worked incredibly well for them. Business owners affected by what was shared with them would reply, someone from their team would fire off a quick reply that usually led to more questions than answers, which eventually leads to a "it might be easier to talk this through over a quick call," which then turns into a new client relationship. All they had to focus on was getting more people on their curation list, and the clients literally came to them.

ALWAYS BE SELLING

Earlier in this chapter I described these educational emails as the "glue" that would allow you to build up enough currency to be able to effectively pull off great pitches. While it's true that these emails aren't tasked to sell, you absolutely should be referencing relevant products or services throughout your educational emails and including soft calls to action within the emails themselves.

Ramit Sethi, author of *I Will Teach You to Be Rich*, runs a large training company that has helped hundreds of thousands of us start a side hustle, find a dream job, and more. When the team sends out their regular newsletter, they include links to a few recommended products in the footer. While they absolutely rotate through live promotions of these products, which is where the bulk of their sales come from, they're also able to get their sales page in front of their readers each and every week. Remember: when *I* might finally be ready to take that next step and buy might not align with when *you* think it's best to actively promote.

Kamil Sethi

P.S. This program also includes our iron-clad, 100% money-back, 60-day guarantee: You can try the ENTIRE program and *then* decide if it's right for you.

Featured Products

Earnable
Learn how to be your own boss, do what you love, and earn more.

Find Your Dream Job
What if you woke up EXCITED to go to work? I show you how to achieve it, step by step.

SuccessTriggers
Ready-to-use mental frameworks for increased happiness, confidence, & success.

I WILL TEACH YOU TO BE RICH
BY *Ramit Sethi*
No guilt, no excuses, no BS. Just a 6-week program that works. Over 1,000,000 copies sold.

The I Will Teach You To Be

SEGMENTATION STILL MATTERS

There are two types of emails where reacting to segmentation *really* matters:

- Your onboarding emails, which we covered in chapter five
- Your pitch emails, which we covered in chapters six and seven

These are the emails tasked with welcoming new people to your audience and showing them that they're at the right place, and convincing them to buy from you. Making these emails highly personal is important.

But you should also try to make your "glue" material, the educational content you're sending in between pitches, as personalized as possible. This can be as simple as just favoring the usage of the phrase "agencies like you" over "freelancers or agencies like you." When sharing an example in a newsletter, try to see if you can come up with a handful of examples that are appropriate for your highest volume segments.

Your subscribers aren't privy to your publishing schedule, and usually aren't weighing whether what they're currently reading of yours is a nurturing email or a sales email. To them it's just another email from your brand. And as we discussed earlier, the job of every email is to get someone engaged and to keep reading. More engagement leads to more people getting value from you, which means more people acting on your calls to action, which leads to more sales and more referrals. The best way to boost engagement is to make your emails more personally relevant, which is what great segmentation and personalization can lead to.

ASKING FOR REFERRALS

You'll recall that when James Clear first launched *Atomic Habits*, his email list was at around four hundred thousand subscribers. Now he has well over two million. While much of his growth can be credited to the success of the book, he's also not leaving it up to chance that his readers share his work.

Here's what James includes at the bottom of every email he sends:

> **Share 3-2-1 and get something useful.**
> If you enjoy these messages, please tell a friend about the 3-2-1 Newsletter. And if you do, I'll send you a special bonus.
> **You're just 3 referrals away from unlocking *The Great Speeches* PDF.**
> For years, I have collected a list of insightful speeches that are not widely known. I've discovered many hidden gems. Recently, I created transcripts for 10 of my favorites and compiled them into a single document titled, "Great Talks Most People Have Never Heard." Each one is filled with useful ideas for life and work.
> *Here's how to get access to it . . .*
> You have a custom referral link (see below). Just copy and paste your referral link into an email, on social media, or however else you'd like to share it. If 3 new people sign up through your link, then you'll automatically get an email with the Great Speeches PDF attached. Thanks for spreading the word.[14]

If you share his email list with three friends, he'll send you an exclusive PDF resource his team has created. He also makes it obvious how easy it is to share ("just copy and paste your referral link into an email, on social media, or however else you'd like to share it"). This allows you to actively incentivize your readers to help fuel your business growth.

Louis Nicholls, one of the founders of SparkLoop,[15] has a lot of data on referral programs. His company is responsible for powering referrals for some of the largest newsletters, and the data he's sitting on is pretty incredible. Here's what Louis had to say when asked about whether it makes sense for a brand to implement a newsletter referral program: *They can often get somewhere between 15 and 20 percent faster growth with a referral program, but the average that we have across our SparkLoop customer base is about 35 percent at the moment, which is just slightly higher than I think* Morning Brew *has."*

When I was describing the L.B.P.S. system, I closed by commenting on how the beauty of the system was that you could set it up *once*, charge it with nurturing new subscribers and pitching them on a recommended product or service, and then focus your email marketing team's effort entirely on getting more people into your L.B.P.S. With a referral program, your entire growth effort begins to compound really nicely. As you get more people into your email system, you're obviously building more trust and scale and increasing sales, but you're also incentivizing your list to share with their network. Growth leads to more growth.

While James Clear's referral program has a single offer—"refer 3 people and get The Great Speeches PDF"—many successful programs offer tiers of offers. Justin Moore of Creator Wizard[16] helps social media influencers find paid brand deals and has built an entire consultancy and training company up around empowering creators. When Justin sends a newsletter, he incentivizes his readers in a few key ways:

- **Tier #1: Refer one person and get access to Secret Brand Deal Research.** Every email he sends showcases a few brands that are looking to partner with creators (these are brands like CVS, Mattel, Bulldog Skincare, and others). But he intentionally ghosts out some exclusive sponsor content, which you only get if you get one fellow creator to join the list.

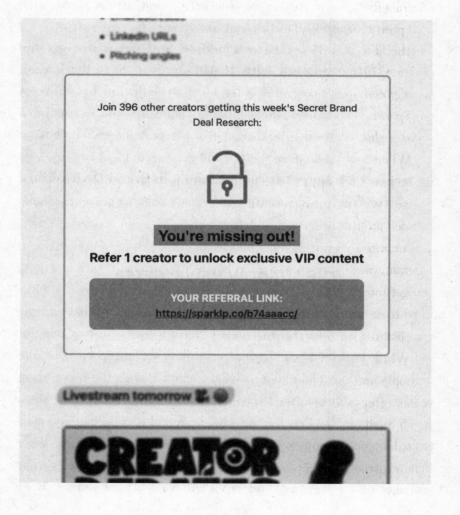

- **Tier #2: Refer five people and get $100 off the Brand Deal Wizard training program.** Every few months, Justin and his team host a live class that teaches creators everything they need to know about working with brands, and they include contract templates and more that help your typical YouTuber appear a lot more professional. If you add five or more people to the list, you get the exclusive content each week *and* $100 off the next live class.

- **Tier #3: Refer fifteen people and get a one-on-one strategy session with Justin.** You can go to the Creator Wizard website and book a call with Justin, but it'll cost $1,000. Or you can get fifteen friends to join the email list, which can easily be done with a few posts on social media or a shout-out in a newsletter, and get it free.

- **Tier #4: Refer fifty people and join Brand Deal Wizard for free.** This is their periodic live class that currently retails for $2,000.

THE SHADOW NEWSLETTER

Most brands are going to be sending educational content that's mostly evergreen. This means that what you have to say is just as relevant today as it will be a year from now. Unless you're reporting on the daily fluctuations of Bitcoin or what's happening in the news, most of what you probably have to share will have a pretty long shelf life.

A Shadow Newsletter is yet one more tool to help you and your team stay out of your email platform. It's an automated newsletter that sends out weekly content to subscribers, soft promotes your products or services, asks for replies to kick off sales discussions when necessary, gets subscribers sharing, and keeps your list nice and warm. The idea is that once you've had someone join your list, and after they've been successfully onboarded via your Immersion Sequence or L.B.P.S., you then pass them into your Shadow Newsletter. This will then continue to nurture them, and every once in a while you pop in with targeted sales promotions.

It might initially seem like the only real benefit to queueing up a newsletter that goes out automatically is that it makes you and your team's life a bit easier. You're not stuck on the "email hamster wheel," responsible for coming up with and sending out new content each and every week. But there's another, possibly more important, reason for considering prescheduled newsletters: *progression.*

Picture somebody new to your brand joining your email list. They're put through your Immersion Sequence, and over the span of about four emails they're given a high-level crash course about what they're getting into, and they're told that every Thursday at around 11 AM they'll be getting something original and useful emailed to them. On the following Thursday, they get your live newsletter. This edition, however, happens to be in the middle of a multipart series. It uses some language that the new reader might not be totally familiar with, and might be a bit advanced considering their relative lack of familiarity with the domain you work in. They're thrown headfirst into whatever your team happens to be sending this week, and what you're sending *might not be what they need to hear.*

A great Shadow Newsletter is going to start with content that focuses on the basics and establishes the ground rules of the problem space you work within. From there, subsequent emails can build off the new understanding that the previous emails created. Think of this like the difference between the blog and a book. I could tear apart this book and turn every key idea in it into a dedicated blog post. Because of how blogs (and the minds that write blog posts) typically work, there wouldn't be much rhyme or reason to the order of these blog posts. And when you arrive at the blog, you'll see a chronologically ordered list of all of my posts—starting with the most recent. If this part of the book was my latest blog post, and I threw around terms like "L.B.P.S." and "Immersion Sequence," you'd probably have no idea what I was talking about.

But the same content, organized into a book, necessarily needs to follow a specific order. Later chapters build on what was said in the earlier chapters. The same should be done with your Shadow Newsletter. Start with the fundamentals and the best, most engaging content you've ever written. You want people to not get overwhelmed by what you're saying, especially if you sometimes come up with pretty advanced material. And you also want your new readers to think that your content is just so incredible that they'd be a fool to ever skip past an email from your brand.

If you're able to, you should also consider possibly having multiple Shadow Newsletters. Depending on *why* someone joined your list, you might want to send them different content initially than you would others. With an eye toward creating the ultimate subscriber experience, what sort of up-front content should someone struggling to lose weight get compared to someone else who's aiming to build muscle?

Chapter 9

BUILD IN THE OPEN

Over the years, I've worked with many clients who hired my company to build large-scale websites. One client—we'll call him "Jim"—had a background in cinema. He was an old-school Hollywood producer, and he wanted us to build a new, highly niched social networking website that he and his wife could run. Jim was such a great guy to work with, but he brought plenty of film baggage. For one thing, he really struggled to internalize that websites weren't ever "final." He was obsessed with making everything perfect. "Fair enough," I thought. Jim came from a world where, once the film was done . . . that was it. You couldn't add new scenes to fill in the gaps that reviewers brought up. It had to be perfect as is.

Jim and I also didn't see eye-to-eye when it came to looping in the readers of his website to give us feedback on the work we were doing. Everything was so secretive. This, again, had to do with his background in film. Plots weren't something openly discussed with fans in his experience. Teaser trailers would be released, but for the most part films were kept hush-hush until right before release date. Modern, online businesses, especially online businesses backed by an engaged list of email subscribers, have a unique advantage. Not only can they learn from their audience, but they can also make their audience collaborators in the success of whatever it is they're doing.

Your email list can, and should, also be used as your brand's internal sounding board. This is a place where you can test new ideas, new products, or ask for feedback and advice. Best of all, since you own the medium and control how people reply back, you don't need to worry about pesky competitors getting access to the data you uncover.

WHY BUILD IN THE OPEN?

It doesn't always come naturally to show "how the sausage is made" to others, especially customers and people that you hope one day become customers! Many brands dream of being like Apple, with fans waiting on the edge of their seats for that *one more thing*. The reality is . . . most of us *aren't* Apple. We're not in an arms race with multibillion-dollar multinational competitors. In fact, if you're a run-of-the-mill small business, you have an advantage that the big corporations don't. You can easily keep your ears to the ground, listen to what you're hearing from your customers and non-customers alike, and iterate fast.

Test Product Ideas

My first training program came about largely by accident. I was actively working on Planscope, and to market the software, we ended up writing a lot of material we thought would be useful for our target audience of freelancers and agencies. We created content about pricing projects, writing proposals, finding new clients, building a team, and other things that we thought the kind of people who would use Planscope might be searching the internet for.

We ended up building a fast-growing email list of people who found our content and joined our opt-in offer, which was a five-day crash course on working with clients. Unfortunately, most of the people we attracted were more interested in our educational content than the project management product we'd built. While the list grew, we started to syndicate the same content we were posting on our website as dedicated emails to the list. And we'd actively ask the list for feedback: Was what we were sharing helpful? What else did they want to learn? Should we go deeper into anything?

Pricing kept coming up. People wanted to charge more, and they were intrigued by this idea called "value-based pricing" that I kept throwing around in the articles I wrote. More content was written on pricing, and more questions kept coming in. Eventually I decided to announce to my list that I was thinking of writing a short e-book on pricing for freelancers. I wasn't quite sure what I'd write about, but if they were interested, I asked them to reply back and let me know what they'd like to see covered.

So many replies came back. And within a day or two, the outline of *Double Your Freelancing Rate* was basically written for us. I got to work—but I first took preorders. It's one thing to say that you're interested, but are you interested enough to order something before it even exists? They were.

Back in 2012, writing and selling e-books online was still something that really was new territory, and the book did great. I was really pleased and thought maybe we could run both a software company and a training company. The training would justify the content creation, and while not everyone was salivating over our project management tool, there were definitely a lot of other requests that we were sitting on.

We kept listening. A lot of what we were hearing was now from people who were freelancers but wanted to grow a team and build an agency. Some just wanted to be able to say they managed a team; others wanted to be able to step away from client work and not have their cash flow dry up; and everyone wanted to make more money for themselves. This led us to decide to put a simple P.S. at the bottom of an upcoming newsletter:

P.S. Do you want to start an agency?

We've had so many people ask us about what it takes to go from being a solo freelancer to creating a team. How do you hire? How do you manage cash flow? What sort of legal concerns do you need to worry about? And most importantly, how do you make sure you have a consistent supply of clients to keep your team busy?

This is something I (Brennan) have done firsthand, and it's something I really haven't written much about yet.

I'm thinking of hosting a two-day live workshop over Google Hangouts. You, me, and 24 others will dig into everything you need to know to make this transition. It'll cost $1,000.

If you're interested, reply to this email and I can send you a bit more about what I'm going to teach. There's no sales page or anything just yet, so the only way to join will be to email me directly.

Dozens of replies came through, and by the end of the day we had sold $25,000 in seats. (This was when Planscope was only making about $3,000 a month.) I knew we were on to something.

I taught the class, and then was able to fill two more classes from just the original interest that first email generated. Then, and only then, did we decide to actually build a website for this live workshop, which we now called *The Consultancy Masterclass*. All in all, we ended up hosting fourteen of these live workshops and made more than $400,000 with them.

Would we have decided to focus on building this without back-and-forth from our audience? Probably not. Would we have probably done what a lot of new course creators do, writing out a full-blown video course, hiring a videographer, and more—and likely ending up with the *wrong* course? Most likely.

Because here's what happened during the course of those fourteen two-day workshops, which took place over about two years: every workshop was better than the previous one. Because these were live discussion-based workshops, we were able to determine where we were losing people, what attendees got really excited about, and what material ended up having the biggest return on investment for our students.

Only after doing this a bunch of times did we feel confident to package it all into a self-serve video course—*the right* video course—that was entirely based on the iterative approach to learning we took in starting, selling, and hosting *The Consultancy Masterclass*.

No matter what kind of business you run or what you're selling, you should do everything you can to:

- **Learn from your audience.** This starts with segmentation, but it really ends up becoming a force to behold when you collate segment data with the raw words, feelings, and pains of your audience.
- **Read between the lines.** Not everything you hear should be taken at face value. What did Henry Ford purport to say (which it seems he actually didn't)? "If I had asked people what they wanted, they would have said a faster horse." By capturing this feedback from your audience, you'll eventually start noticing trends and be able to get to the root of what people *really* need from you.
- **Don't obsess over perfection.** Collaborate with your audience. Iterate quickly, and don't be afraid to backtrack. If people feel like they played a part in the ideation or creation of something, they'll want to own it once it's available. They'll also want to tell all their friends about it.

BUILD EXCITEMENT AND ANTICIPATION

After you have a product or service that you're working toward, I find that there are usually very few downsides to sharing what you're learning along the way.

In 2012, Nathan Barry had successfully carved out a nice living for himself selling courses and e-books online. His products, like *The App Design Handbook* and *Designing Web Applications*, along with regular blog posts and email newsletters on design and entrepreneurship, rewarded him with an audience of design-focused entrepreneurs. These were people who were wanting to, or actively in the process of, carving out a living online for themselves.

But Nathan wanted to do something bigger and bolder than just creating digital training products and selling them. He publicly challenged himself to create a software company that would be making $5,000 a month within the first six months. The article, released at the end of 2012, was titled "Starting the Web App Challenge: From Zero to $5,000/Month in 6 Months."

He kicked off his public announcement to his audience by talking about how far he'd come, but also the limitation of the business he'd created thus far: "My last two projects, both books, have been insanely successful. Selling more than $80,000 worth in just over 3 months. The connections I've made, marketing lessons learned, and financial freedom I now have make a huge difference. There is only one problem: those were all one-time sales."

He continued the article by detailing more about how great it was to have all the freedom that comes with working on the internet and making pretty great money by genuinely delivering lots of free and paid value to an audience. And then he introduced the challenge on his website.[17]

> I could just start a new web app and work on it quietly for a year before launching, but where is the fun in that? Writing and launching *Designing Web Applications* in only three months taught me that if I compress the deadlines I can meet a goal much more quickly. So here is the challenge:
>
> Within six months build a web application to $5,000 in recurring revenue each month. A friend just referred to that timeline as "aggressive" so let's add some more restrictions to make it more difficult:

- I am starting without an idea. So I don't know what the application will be, what it will do, or who it is targeted towards.
- I can only spend $5,000 of my own money in this entire process. Meaning all other funds necessary have to come from paying customers. Since I will be hiring out the development, getting paying customers right away is mandatory.
- I cannot spend more than 20 hours a week on this project. If allowed, I waste tons of time on projects. This limit is partially because there are other things that need my time (contract projects, writing, etc.) and to help keep me focused.

The best part of this is that I am going to be completely transparent about every step of the process. Follow along on this blog to hear how things are going, what I'm learning, and the mistakes you shouldn't repeat. The deadline is July 1st, 2013 to have $5,000 a month worth of paying customers. That could be 50 customers paying $100 a month, 10 customers paying $500 a month, or somewhere in the middle (most likely). Think I can do it? Good. Me too.

A little help.

I want to do everything possible to remove risk and make this project successful. So I've asked my friend Brennan Dunn to be an official advisor to my web app challenge. It's not very official really, but he will be there to answer questions, help me choose a developer, and help me work through marketing strategies.

> Brennan has been a Rails developer for years and runs his own project management web application called Planscope. Since Brennan did all the design, development, and marketing of Planscope himself, he has already solved many of the problems I will probably face. I expect his advice to be very helpful.

(You might notice someone you "know" mentioned above!)

Over the next few months, Nathan was an open book about what he was doing. He shared what was working. What wasn't. He talked about how miserable it was to see revenue stagnate month after month. He shared what it was like to build a product (in this case, an email marketing platform) and have it break and affect the real businesses of his customers. His transparency led to more people who wanted to follow his journey. This attention also booked Nathan on more podcasts, opened up speaking opportunities, and more—all of which grew his audience.

He even shared his revenue numbers on a public dashboard. Anyone could see how many customers they had, what they made per customer, and so on. While some people questioned Nathan's judgment in being so fiscally transparent, he continued to forge ahead. He knew that if he helped people, people would help him.

The *Web App Challenge* ended up working. Really well. Today ConvertKit makes more than $2.5 million a month and was recently valued at over $200 million. Sixty-four people work for ConvertKit, and over forty thousand companies are subscribed as customers. Largely thanks to an ongoing commitment to build in the open.

Chapter 10

THE NEW ROLE OF SOCIAL MEDIA

This might just be the shortest chapter in this entire book. But, alas, this *is* a book about all the virtues and moneymaking opportunities that come with email marketing.

However, I'm not so much of a curmudgeon to think that there's no use for social media. I'm pretty active on Twitter and Facebook and have used both to grow my various businesses. And just about every business I've cited in this book has a large social media presence.

Plus, you only need to look as far as someone like Kat Norton, also known as "Miss Excel," who runs a Microsoft Office training company that regularly sells more than six figures a day in courses— *entirely through TikTok*. You can do incredibly well on social media. I'm just not your guy for that (plus, you wouldn't want to watch me gyrate and sing on camera).

Social media definitely has its uses. Plenty of great resources and books on how to grow your follower count, game each platform's algorithm, and so on are out there. But like I mentioned early on in this book, my biggest beef with social media platforms is the lack of ownership and portability: you *don't* ever own your following. You have zero control over the whims of the platform's algorithm. And no social media exists that makes delivering personalized one-to-one feeds of communication possible.

But I want to talk strategically about how social media fits into the playbook I've outlined so far. Let's look at a few strategies.

ACQUISITION

Social media platforms like Twitter make it easy to share bite-sized content, and for people who like that content to help propel it along by deciding to reshare it to their followers. Twitter's also in the business of trying to get as many of their users as possible to *keep* using the platform. So, even when you decide to "like" a tweet, there's a good chance—assuming the tweet ends up getting plenty of likes—that it'll be pushed into non-follower feeds thanks to Twitter's discovery engine.

One example of using Twitter to build an email list is from the duo Dickie Bush and Nicolas Cole, who help people create a writing habit. They've created an internal system for posting on both Twitter and LinkedIn that's optimized to get people *off* Twitter and on to their email list. Here's how they describe this system:[18]

- **[Attraction]** Create free, valuable content on one to two social platforms.
- **[Retention]** Drive a percent of that attention to an email list (where you deepen the relationship you have with readers—and continue to prove you're the right person to learn from).
- **[Monetization]** Some percent of those engaged readers will then go on to buy products from you.

That's it.

That's the whole business, in a nutshell.

Which means, part of your [Attraction] Content Strategy is educating people on all the things they can do/use to [Retention] deepen their relationship with you.

How they actually do this is really smart. They're already sharing so much great information with their audience privately, over email. They simply extract highlights (for example, "7 copywriting mistakes that are hurting your sale") from what they send to their list, along with deep dives into key ideas and topics, and deliver a bite-sized representation of what they teach extensively over email and to their customers. Their posts are so good, and so concise, that they regularly get thousands of likes whenever they share anything on social media.

Dickie and Nicolas don't just want to share *interesting* ideas; they want what they're sharing to actually lead to the results they care about—specifically new email list subscribers and new customers. They explain:

The big idea here is that if we are going to spend the time to create so much content on Twitter & LinkedIn, then we want to make sure it's actively building our business at the same time. (A lot of people—ourselves included—assume this "just happens," but it wasn't until we sat down and really went through this process that we realized how we've basically spent a year and a half barely plugging our own stuff. Through a business lens, that's a problem.)[19]

They're on a path to building their email list to over one hundred thousand fans and customers. They have some of the best material I've come across for building a writing habit and have already helped thousands of paying customers. Since they're such a small team, they know that most of their time needs to be spent researching and developing their products, supporting their customers, and spending as much time working *on* the business as possible.

But they couldn't ignore social media, which has helped them build the business they have today. They created a system, their Content Cadence, and follow an internal playbook that spells out exactly what to post to social media and when, and what to promote with each post (e.g., their newsletter). This lets their team spend as little time as possible on social media while maximizing the rewards they get from it:

> We know what we want to build Ship 30 for 30 into, and what products we want to launch next, and that requires us to dedicate as much of our headspace as possible working in that direction. However, as a digital business, we don't really have the luxury of "not caring" about Twitter or LinkedIn since those two platforms are what educate people on why they should become a Digital Writer, launch digital products, and take the Ship 30 for 30 challenge. So creating this Content Cadence was really a way for us to keep our social engines running (and growing), but also do so in a sustainable way that allows us to have more time to build products and our business.[20]

IT'S (OFTEN) EASIER TO ENGAGE

There are a lot of reasons why you should encourage your audience to reply to your emails. It's a great way to learn from your audience and get, in their own words, a wealth of invaluable data about who you're serving. It also sends a positive signal to email servers. They interpret replies as a vote of confidence for the legitimacy of the sender, which helps with overall email deliverability.

Yet replying to a brand's email can be daunting for many. What isn't as difficult is engaging with a brand on social media. After all, social media is made for engagement. It's *easy* to post a comment. It's *trivial* to like or love a post. And because social is, well, social, other people can chime in and support what you have to say. You know you're not shouting to the void on social media, whereas you might feel like that's what's happening if you reply to a brand's weekly newsletter.

One way to both add a bit of discoverability to your emails *and* to encourage dialogue with your audience is to use "Click to Tweet" links in your emails.[21]

The Spectator, a weekly British periodical, knows that their readers love their cartoons. Whenever they send their daily email newsletter to subscribers, they include a simple "Tweet This Cartoon" button under each cartoon. Whoever does the sharing has free will to amend the canned tweet however they'd like—maybe they add their own spin, comment on how stupid the cartoon is, praise it for being all too accurate. But, most importantly for *The Spectator*, someone who *isn't* on their social media team just willingly promoted something of theirs, and this promotion also included a handy sign-up link for their newsletter.

MANY-TO-MANY VERSUS ONE-TO-ONE

When you send an email out using your email marketing software, the messages that land in the inboxes of your subscribers come from *you* and replies go to *you*. Even though that same email campaign might be going out to millions of others, the people on the receiving end have no idea who else is learning from you and who else is also struggling with the same problems they're facing.

While email will never truly be social, there's no reason you can't find ways of getting your audience to talk peer-to-peer amongst themselves. Jay Clouse, a writer and podcaster, challenged his audience to make marketing themselves on social media second nature. He coined the hashtag #tweet100 and encouraged readers to use that hashtag when executing on the challenge. Now anyone in Jay's audience—along with anyone on the sidelines—could see how others like them were taking action thanks to Jay.

Another common pattern is to mirror any educational content you send to your email list to your company's blog. Val Geisler, a former customer retention consultant who's since moved on to the greener pastures of software, would email her list "teardowns" of how different software companies onboarded their new customers using email. These public teardowns were a bit like what she'd provide clients who hired her, and included her recommendations on what to keep, what to cut, and other areas for improvement. The difference? They were public, and the companies she tore down didn't hire Val, but those of us who have a lot riding on the success of our software's onboarding could use these educational teardowns to get an idea of what it might be like to work with Val.

The emails sent didn't include the entire teardown within them. That wouldn't make much sense, especially since these reviews were laden with lots of images and had some formatting requirements that made them better suited to be shown as a web page. She'd link to the teardown on her website and ask her readers to comment on the article with what they thought and if she missed anything in her analysis. This gave her readers a way to share their feedback with Val and led to every teardown being framed more as a discussion between students of software onboarding (led by Val, of course), rather than just Val pontificating from on high.

Conclusion

COMMUNITY OVER COMPANY

If you act on the advice in this book, you will begin to shift away from one-size-fits-all thinking toward giving customers exactly what they're asking for: personalized, relevant, and authentic value.

These ideas work. I've seen it consulting with companies, running RightMessage, and teaching tens of thousands of marketers and business owners how to build a better business through tasteful email automation and personalization. Some of the technology may be new, but the approach has been successful since humans first bartered with shells and other trinkets. People want to know: "What's in it for me?" and "Why should I buy from you / change my thinking / accept your proposal to date you?"

This Is Personal is personal for me. I live and work by these principles. It's not just about sending better emails.

Here are just a few more ways that brands are using this framework to build better, more profitable relationships with their audiences:

— *Authors use email to cut out the middleman, the retail stores, and have a direct line of communication with their readers. Josh Kaufman, the author of The Personal MBA, asks new* readers to forward a picture of their purchase receipt to a special email address he's set up. This delivers some additional resources that can't be bundled in a book (e.g., videos and PDF worksheets), and also allows him to talk with his readers. The books he's written since have largely come from what Josh has learned from his list.

- *Bariatric surgeons use personalized email campaigns to guide people through a very long decision-making process.* Jonah Selner provides "done-for-you" email consulting for surgeons. When it comes to bariatric surgery, it typically takes around two years for someone to go from potentially interested to actually booked in for surgery. The slow-release email campaigns that he provides his clients allow patients to educate themselves on the pros and cons of bariatric surgery, proactively answers any questions they might have, provides past success stories, and more. The average salesperson wouldn't want to check in with a would-be customer for multiple years, but email doesn't care.

- *Independently owned bakeries are using personalized email marketing to sell lots of cakes.* Tammy Youngerwood runs Jerusalem Cake Design. She segments her audience by the kind of cakes they like, allergens, and so on. When she whips together new, delicious creations, she's able to quickly spin up and send targeted campaigns to her community.

- *A heavy metal band uses email to connect with fans and raise funding.* Most of us might listen to artists we love through Spotify and find out that they're going to be playing in our city thanks to casually checking out Ticketmaster, but Ryan Baustert of the band Throw the Fight encourages fans to join their list and sends segmented email campaigns depending on where people live to promote upcoming appearances. They've also been able to raise over $15,000 from their fans—entirely over email.

— *The State of Washington and Explore Washington State are sending highly targeted email campaigns based on travel goals and interests.* Scott Cowan shared that Explore Washington State is segmenting new subscribers to their newsletter based on their interests (for example, food and drink, fun with kids, etc.). Their weekly newsletter then becomes increasingly more tailored and relevant based on someone's interests.

It's about being a positive force in the lives of your customers.

How do you make your business more about your audience and their needs and less about you and what you want to sell them? How do you turn "people who buy from you" into a community? Your customers are more than just sales targets. You can learn from them. You can teach and inspire them. If you truly help them, they'll be loyal to you forever.

Acknowledgments

This book would not have been possible without the support and contribution of a few key people.

First, there's my wife, Laura. I set about writing this book while she was pregnant and finished it with a toddler running around our house. She patiently put up with me amidst the many late-night writing sessions and all the frantic deadlines I had to adhere to.

Lisa DiMona, my agent, and David Moldawer, who initially helped me with the foundations of this book, helped a novice author like me figure out how to translate a rough, highly technical set of marketing concepts into something that can truly benefit a lot of companies.

I'd also like to thank all the friends and colleagues of mine who lent so much of their time and not only helped me develop the core thesis of this book, but also contributed to the content inside. Shai Schechter at RightMessage, Nathan Barry of ConvertKit, Amy Hoy and Alex Hillman of 30x500, André Chaperon, Jay Clouse, Shawn Blanc, Justin Moore, Josh Kaufman, Patrick McKenzie, and so many others greatly helped make this book a reality.

And, finally, to tens of thousands of readers and customers of mine. I've learned so much from so many of you over the last decade.

Notes

1. *Mac Address*. YouTube. Accessed November 6, 2022. https://www
   .youtube.com/c/macaddress.
2. "Discover the World's Best Service & Software Providers." 99firms.
   Accessed November 6, 2022. https://99firms.com/blog/how-many
   -email-users-are-there/#gref.
3. "Creating Passionate Users." Creating Passionate Users. Accessed
   November 6, 2022. https://headrush.typepad.com/.
4. "Making Content Meaningful to Users." Creating Passionate Users.
   Accessed November 6, 2022. https://headrush.typepad.com/creating
   _passionate_users/2005/01/we_should_all_t.html.
5. Flynn, Pat. "The Smart Passive Income Blog—Smart Ways to Live a
   Passive Income Lifestyle on the Internet with SmartPassiveIncome
   .com." Smart Passive Income, November 3, 2022. https://www.smart
   passiveincome.com/.
6. Sumo Group, Inc. "Email Signup Benchmarks: How Many Visitors
   Should Be Converting." Sumo. Accessed November 6, 2022. https://
   sumo.com/stories/email-signup-benchmarks.
7. Rosenberg, Matthew, Nicholas Confessore, and Carole Cadwalladr.
   "How Trump Consultants Exploited the Facebook Data of Millions."
   New York Times, March 17, 2018. https://www.nytimes.com/2018/03
   /17/us/politics/cambridge-analytica-trump-campaign.html.
8. Hollatz, Kayla. "How 'Quiz Funnel Queen' Chanti Zak Generated
   $50,000 from a Quiz." *Interact Blog*, May 23, 2022. https://www
   .tryinteract.com/blog/quiz-funnel-interview-with-chanti-zak/.

9. Sumo Group, Inc. "Email Signup Benchmarks."

10. Ibid; Dean, Brian. "How to Boost Conversions by 785% in One Day (the Content Upgrade)." Backlinko, September 2, 2016. https://backlinko.com/increase-conversions.

11. Chappell, Sophie-Grace. "Plato on Knowledge in the *Theaetetus*." Stanford Encyclopedia of Philosophy. November 21, 2019. https://plato.stanford.edu/entries/plato-theaetetus/.

12. "No-Nonsense Nutrition and Training Guides." RippedBody.com, August 24, 2022. https://rippedbody.com/.

13. "Convince Your Boss—SMASHINGCONF Online Workshops." Accessed November 6, 2022. https://smashingconf.com/pdf/convince-your-boss-sf.pdf.

14. "3-2-1 Thursday Newsletter." James Clear, October 27, 2022. https://jamesclear.com/3-2-1.

15. "The #1 Newsletter Growth Platform." SparkLoop. Accessed November 6, 2022. https://sparkloop.app/.

16. https://www.creatorwizard.com/.

17. Barry, Nathan. "Starting the Web App Challenge: From Zero to $5,000/Month in 6 Months." Nathan Barry website, March 10, 2015. https://nathanbarry.com/starting-web-app-challenge/.

18. Bush, Dickie and Nicolas Cole. "Our Content Strategy to Grow Our Email List to 100k." Start Writing Online in 30 Days—Ship 30 for 30. https://www.ship30for30.com/post/our-content-strategy-to-grow-our-email-list-to-100k.

19. Ibid.

20. Ibid.

21. Hussain, Anum. "How to Generate Click-to-Tweet Links for Your Content [Quick Tip]." *HubSpot Blog*, February 1, 2017. https://blog.hubspot.com/marketing/how-to-generate-click-to-tweet-links-cta-quick-tip-ht.

Index

About the Author

Photo by Claire Dyer

Brennan Dunn is the co-founder of Right-Message, a software company that helps companies segment their audience and personalize for their marketing, and the founder of Create & Sell, a training platform for all things email marketing. Throughout his career, he's been trying to find creative ways to bridge together "one size fits all" online messaging with the sort of highly personalized, one-on-one sales discussions he mastered in his former life of owning an agency. He lives in England with his wife and daughters.